THE BACH CELLO SUITES

Steven Isserlis enjoys a unique and multifaceted career as soloist, chamber musician and educator. He appears regularly with the world's leading orchestras, gives recitals every season in major musical centres, devises fascinating chamber music programmes, performs with period instrument ensembles, enjoys giving concerts for children and works with many contemporary composers. He has written two children's books and gives masterclasses worldwide. For the past twenty-five years he has been Artistic Director of the International Musicians' Seminar at Prussia Cove, Cornwall. Steven Isserlis's Hyperion recording of the Bach cello suites met with universal critical acclaim.

Further praise for *The Bach Cello Suites*:

'This is a very important book indeed. One of the best of its kind. Written by a real musician, who understands and loves Bach and his wonderful compositions. Bravo!' Sir András Schiff

'It's both informal and at the same time totally serious; it's the work of a witty and eloquent musician who knows both the instrument and the music with perfect familiarity, yet who never loses sight of the sheer astonishment his music evokes in the listener, the grandeur and the almost supernatural strangeness of something both so human and so profound. All great music should be lucky enough to find such a guide and companion.' Philip Pullman

'An accessible, eloquent guide to the world's greatest – and maybe most elusive – pieces of music. And written by the man I'd want to tell me about it. This is such a delight.' Derren Brown

'Fascinating . . . Isserlis, as a distinguished performer of the suites, has the insight and the authority to consider what, and how.' Paul Griffiths, *Times Literary Supplement*

'Steven Isserlis is one of the world's great cellists, and his recordings of the Bach cello suites in 2007 were critically acclaimed for the integrity of their interpretation. Now he brings that insight to bear in a highly engaging book "for music lovers of all shapes and sizes". From a brief biography of Bach, through the historical context and emotional significance of the suites, Isserlis produces an illuminating, accessible and detailed analysis of one of Bach's seminal works.' Hannah Beckerman, *Observer*

by the same author
WHY BEETHOVEN THREW THE STEW
WHY HANDEL WAGGLED HIS WIG
ROBERT SCHUMANN'S ADVICE TO YOUNG MUSICIANS

The Bach Cello Suites

A Companion

STEVEN ISSERLIS

faber

First published in the UK and the USA in 2021
by Faber & Faber Ltd
The Bindery, 51 Hatton Garden,
London ECIN 8HN

This paperback edition first published in 2023

Typeset by Faber & Faber Ltd
Printed in the UK by CPI Group (UK) Ltd, Croydon, CR0 4YY

A CIP record for this book
is available from the British Library

ISBN 978-0-571-36625-5

Printed and bound in the UK on FSC® certified paper in line with our continuing
commitment to ethical business practices, sustainability and the environment.
For further information see faber.co.uk/environmental-policy

2 4 6 8 10 9 7 5 3

To David Waterman (a.k.a. Uncle Silly)
with thanks for over forty-five years
– and counting – of close friendship

Contents

Introduction

This book is intended for music-lovers of all shapes and sizes, ranging from the casual listener to the performing musician. My simple aim is to amplify, if possible, the enjoyment and understanding of those listening to Bach's cello suites by offering my own, very personal, observations on the music. Everyone who loves the suites will have his or her own views, which may be radically different from mine; that's fine – as it should be, in fact. Mine are constantly changing, and will continue to do so long after this book is in print – again, that is to be expected. Music as all-encompassing as this can be heard, seen, thought of, felt in an infinite variety of ways. My hope, ultimately, is that these reflections on the suites will be taken for what they are intended to be: a continuation of a discussion that will endure for as long as we listen to music – as well as an act of homage to some of the greatest works ever composed.

I am no musicologist, and am deeply grateful to the authors of the many articles and books that have helped me form an overview of the history and provenance of the suites. This is not in any way an academic tome. If the reader can read music, so much the better; but it is not essential. There is, in a few places, some very basic analysis of key moments within the suites, because that was the only way I could find to describe those passages; but those analyses are short – and can be easily skipped, if they're not to your taste. A glossary – to be glossed over, perhaps – is provided at the end of the book.

This is not really a volume to be read all at once, but rather one to be used as a friendly companion before or after listening to (or playing) the suites. Or in the case of Part 6, perhaps even – horrors! How dare I suggest anything so sacrilegious? – while doing so. Shame on me – I'd better begin the book proper forthwith, before I further offend the God of Music that is Bach.

The Magic of the Suites

It is extraordinary how Bach's cello suites, largely unknown for some two hundred years after their composition, have now captured the imaginations, minds and hearts of music-lovers all over the world. For cellists they represent a musical bible; for listeners, scarcely less. They are discussed, ana-lysed, made the subject of fantasies, arguments and quarrels, appropriated by players of countless other instruments; and yet despite this overkill, and perhaps heightened by the lack of a manuscript in Bach's hand or any definite information about the circumstances of their composition, they maintain their air of pristine mystery.

The slightly frustrating thing about this sense of an in-scrutable secret is that the suites themselves really *aren't* that mysterious. They consist primarily of dance music, readily communicative, not especially complex; Bach, unlike some composers, did not seek to hide his message under a veil of convolution. It is, above all, deeply human music, telling an emotional story that should be easy to understand. So many editions (well over a hundred), so many recordings (well over two hundred) and too many words (probably millions) have somehow obscured the clarity of these wonderfully dir-ect works. (This, of course, is why I've recorded the suites and am writing this book. Hmm. At least I've never done – and shall never do – an edition!) Is there a story behind the suites? Just possibly (more on that later). But above all, they consist of pure, unbelievably beautiful music, written by an eminently practical composer for the most basic of forces: one player on four strings, with a bow. They are inexhaustibly moving, because that composer was an incomparable genius who mastered every genre to which he turned his attention, blessed with a (musical) heart and vision that overflowed with just about every emotion known to man or woman – except, perhaps, for embarrassment . . .

As you can probably gather from the above, my reaction to the suites is essentially an instinctive one. Of course, I study and read about them endlessly; every scrap of knowledge can help form an interpretation, and may perhaps add conviction to one's performance. Ultimately, though, the truth lies within the music, not in anything outside it; and it is chiefly the emotional/dramatic/spiritual narrative of the suites, taking us on a vast journey, from peaceful meditation through deepest suffering to radiant exaltation, that I intend to examine here.

First of all, however, some history, most of which I have gleaned, magpie-like, from various distinguished scholars. And a most fascinating – if at times bewildering – history it is . . .

THE STORY

PART 1

J. S. Bach: A very brief biography

Johann Sebastian Bach was born in the town of Eisenach
(where Martin Luther had attended school about 190 years
earlier) in 1685, on what was then 21 March but now, thanks
to the change to the Gregorian calendar, answers to the
name of 31 March. Bach's family were almost all musicians;
particularly appropriate, since their surname – aside from
meaning 'brook' – is one of the few that can be entirely converted into musical notes (in the German system the letter
B is used for the note we know as B flat, the letter H for our
B natural). Orphaned before the age of ten, little Bach was
taken in by an elder brother, Johann Christoph, an organist, who made a start on J. S.'s musical education; it can be
assumed that the latter was a more than willing pupil. The
obituary published a few years after Bach's death – written
by Johann Friedrich Agricola, a musical theoretician, in col-
laboration with the most famous of Bach's four renowned
composer sons, Carl Philipp Emanuel – tells us a rather
charming, if sad, story. Shortly after commencing his studies, little Johann Sebastian longed to play more challenging
pieces than those his brother was giving him. Having espied
a manuscript volume of promising-looking keyboard works
belonging to Johann Christoph, he begged to be allowed to

learn them. His brother sternly prohibited it, and shut the volume away in a bookshelf secured with a latticed front. He had not reckoned, however, with the delicacy of little Bach's hands; waiting until his brother was safely in bed, Johann Sebastian would steal up to the cupboard, push his fingers through the small holes, roll up the volume and extract it. Although he was not allowed a candle of his own (his brother sounds as strict as any father), he would copy the music on nights during which the moon shone through his window. Alas, scarcely had he completed the mammoth task, which had taken him six months, when Johann Christoph found out, and as a punishment hid both original and copy; our Bach had to wait many years, until after his brother's lamented death, before he could recover them.

Despite this setback, J. S.'s musical studies must have progressed brilliantly, and in 1703 he was engaged for his first proper job, as organist in the town of Arnstadt. It cannot be said to have gone smoothly, however. Bach was perhaps not the ideal employee: aside from his gripes about the musical idiocies of the town council, he managed during this time to get into an unseemly brawl with a bassoonist, who accused him of having insulted both his playing and his instrument; to take three months' unauthorised leave; to quarrel with various students; and – ahem – to be accused of inviting a 'stranger maiden' to make music (!) in the church. (In later life, Bach forbade the telling of many stories from his early life. I wonder what else happened?) Furthermore, the council complained that at the organ Bach 'mingled many strange tones' to the chorale, thereby confusing the congregation. It must have been rather a relief to some of the Arnstadt councillors, if not to the music-lovers, when in 1707 Bach resigned and went to take up a new job in nearby Mühlhausen. Here, once his new employers had mastered his admittedly complicated surname (in the first of the few surviving documents they call him Herr Pach, in the second Herr Bache), things seem to have gone better. Nevertheless, the following year he accepted a more lucrative and prestigious offer of employment in a major town, Weimar, where he was to remain until 1717. Despite the brevity of Bach's stay in Mühlhausen, one very important event in his life occurred there: he married his second cousin, Maria Barbara Bach.

Bach's life in Weimar appears to have been busy and successful: originally appointed as court organist and 'chamber musician', he was further honoured within a few years by the title of 'Konzertmeister'. He was also paid to repair smaller keyboard instruments, and particularly to inspect the many organs being built or overhauled at churches in the area; moreover, he was becoming well known as a teacher. On the personal front, six of his children were born in Weimar (though that includes a pair of short-lived twins); these included the composers Wilhelm Friedemann and Carl Philipp Emanuel. He was on friendly terms with many musical celebrities (Georg Philipp Telemann stood as godfather to C. P. E. Bach); and he was mentioned in print for the first time, by Handel's old friend/enemy Johann Mattheson (1681–1764). Many cantatas, and much of his organ music, were written during these years. Alas, after the death of his original employer, things gradually deteriorated, and late in 1717, Bach demanded to be released from his position, in somewhat tactless fashion – and was put in prison for almost a month. It can't have been pleasant – and presumably the children were traumatised; but he was eventually freed, and dismissed in disgrace. Now he was at liberty to accept an even more lucrative offer (like most of the great composers, Bach was quite fond of money), at the court of Köthen.

Here his employer was Prince Leopold, who was passionate about music; he sang, and played the violin, viola da gamba and harpsichord. Bach and Leopold were on such good terms that the prince agreed to be godfather to the last of Bach's children with Maria Barbara, a boy auspiciously named Leopold Augustus (though sadly the infant did not profit from the name, perishing within a year). Even though religious compositions were rarely required, owing to the Prince being Calvinist (meaning that services were conducted without music) – and despite the lack of fine organs in the town – the position in Köthen seems to have been excellent for Bach. His appointment was as Kapellmeister, a step up from his positions in Weimar, and he seems to have been properly appreciated at last. Most of the few cantatas he wrote here were to celebrate birthdays and other festive occasions; but he was able to produce a large body of instrumental masterpieces that were – outwardly, at any rate – secular in character. It was here that he wrote, or at least completed, the works for solo violin (by 1720) and, by extension, presumably the cello suites; the 'Brandenburg' concertos; probably most of the first book of *The Well-Tempered Clavier*; and much else.

But tragedy was to strike: in the summer of 1720, having accompanied his employer while Leopold took the waters at Karlsbad, Bach returned to find that his wife Maria Barbara had died in his absence, and was already buried. (This may perhaps have inspired him to compose the monumental Chaconne that concludes his D minor Partita for solo violin.) By the following year, however, life was already looking up; on 3 December 1721, he married his second wife, Anna Magdalena Wilcke, a singer who was twenty years his junior. It can be assumed that Bach celebrated in style, since he purchased three barrels of wine for the occasion. From the few hints one can glean from the scanty surviving correspondence, Anna Magdalena sounds wonderful: an accomplished and celebrated singer who gave frequent concerts with her husband, as well as copying out much of his music; a lover of plants and birds; and – one can conjecture – a kind stepmother, as well as loving mother. To assist her musical education, Bach compiled two generous volumes, known as the 'Notebooks for Anna Magdalena Bach' – mostly keyboard pieces, mingled with some vocal works. Anna Magdalena also, in her spare time, gave birth to no fewer than thirteen children – of whom, alas, only six survived into adulthood.

It seems, as far as we can tell, to have been an immensely happy marriage – as, we are told, Bach's first marriage had also been. Unfortunately, on the professional side, life was less rosy. Just eight days after Bach's wedding, his employer (like Bach the first time around) married his cousin, the Princess Friderica; alas, she had no interest in music. From this point on, Bach's relationship with Leopold seems to have deteriorated, and it is no surprise that in 1722 Bach should have applied for a vacant post in the great city of Leipzig. In a way, it was a downgrade, since he would be Kantor rather than Kapellmeister here (although he did officially retain his title of Kapellmeister of Köthen until Leopold's death in 1728); but still, the role of Kantor at the Thomasschule – the school associated with the famous Thomaskirche – was significant by almost any standard, with duties far more varied and challenging than those at any of his previous tenures. He was by no means first choice for the post, the city council accepting him only unwillingly, after more 'prestigious' candidates, such as Telemann, had withdrawn. (The councillors even had the cheek to say that 'since the best could not be obtained, mediocre ones would have to be accepted'.) Nevertheless – after emerging with flying colours from a religious examination conducted by two tough professors of theology – Bach was eventually offered the job, one of the bigwigs expressing the fervent hope that Bach's music would not be 'too theatrical'. In May 1723, Bach and his family – including by now the first of Anna Magdalena's children – made their grand entrance into Leipzig in two carriages, preceded by their luggage carried in four wagons. (I hope that the councillor who worried about Bach's theatrical tendencies wasn't watching.)

Predictably, Bach's relations with his employers were less than perfect, but it is with Leipzig, where he was to remain for the rest of his life, that we chiefly associate him. He worked unimaginably hard, often producing a cantata a week, and for several years giving weekly concerts at a local coffee-house; tuning all the instruments of his orchestra, and leading the group from the violin or harpsichord; dazzling audiences and congregations with his organ-playing; training and conducting the choir from the Thomasschule, and giving instrumental lessons to some of them; travelling around to inspect organs in various towns; playing and singing with his family, as well as teaching them and many private pupils; working as musical director for the famous local university; acting as host for large entertainments, if one is to judge from the amount of crockery and cutlery he owned (C. P. E. Bach writes that no eminent musician would pass through Leipzig without visiting the household – 'his house was like a beehive, and just as full of life'); getting involved with both the design and dissemination of new instruments (including, towards the end of his life, Gottfried Silbermann's new fortepiano, which Bach praised and also helped to improve through his perceptive criticisms); taking care of his own instruments – we are told that nobody could tune a harpsichord or clavichord to his satisfaction other than himself; and above all, of course, composing, composing, composing – endlessly. It is said that it would take someone many years of twenty-four-hour-per-day labour just to write out the music Bach left behind – even leaving aside the plethora of missing works. Alongside around two hundred surviving cantatas (and undoubtedly many more than that, since a fair proportion of them have been lost), it was in Leipzig that he wrote, among innumerable other masterpieces, the *St John* and *St Matthew* Passions; most of the works for solo harpsichord and many for organ; oratorios and concertos; and, later, the 'Goldberg' variations, *The Musical Offering*, *The Art of Fugue* and the Mass in B minor. And yet he found time – and energy! – during these Leipzig years to do his bit towards co-producing twelve further children with Anna Magdalena. Miraculous.

After twenty-seven years of these unparalleled achievements, Bach died from a stroke, blind (probably from diabetes) and presumably exhausted, on 28 July 1750. He was buried in Leipzig but, shockingly, soon lay largely forgotten; it was not until 1894 that the body – a body – was exhumed, from a site held by tradition to be the resting-place of the great Kantor, and subsequently buried for all to see and worship at the front of the (much-altered) Thomaskirche. The only slight problem is that it may not be Bach at all . . .

In general, the story of Bach's life and his subsequent reputation is not without controversy: it throws shame on some, glory on others. Shame on those who were so cavalier with his music as to have allowed so many of his works to be lost – probably around a hundred cantatas, many concertos and other instrumental works, and at least one Passion – as well as the manuscripts of countless pieces, including that of the cello suites; shame on critics and writers, from Bach's contemporary Johann Adolph Scheibe onwards, who have accused him of writing turgid, over-intellectual music (can't they hear the profound humanity, the fathomless compassion, the lovable humour?); much shame on the Leipzig councillors, who described him as 'incorrigible' and were already auditioning potential successors for his job the year before Bach actually died*; shame on those behind the decision to destroy – as late as 1903 – the buildings of the Thomasschule in which Bach lived and worked; and shame on those who did nothing for Bach's impoverished last surviving child, Regina Susanna, who lived until 1809. (One of those who eventually tried to rectify this was Beethoven, who wanted to help 'the daughter of the Immortal God of Harmony', as he put it.) Glory, on the other hand, to Johann Nikolaus Forkel – musician, author and the so-called 'father of musicology' – for putting so much work into research for his pioneering biography of Bach; glory to Carl Philipp Emanuel, who seems to have made the most effort of all the children to preserve his father's legacy. (The other sons were perhaps a bit less respectful; Johann Christian, the youngest son, was even said to have referred to his father as 'The Old Wig' – one hopes it was affectionate-ly meant. And possibly explained by the fact that his father apparently described him as 'stupid' – also, one *hopes*, affec-tionately said . . . In any case, Mozart was very fond of J. C. Bach, so he can't have been all bad.) Glory too to Baron van Swieten (1733–1803), early patron of C. P. E., who introduced Mozart, and presumably Haydn, to the music of J. S. Bach and Handel; glory to Felix Mendelssohn, whose passionate championship of Bach's music, and whose revival of the *St Matthew Passion* in Berlin in 1829, when he was just twenty years old, proved a turning point; and, much later, glory to the

---

* Bach wasn't always charming to them either, it must be admitted; in one rather shocking letter, for instance, he complains that the healthy winds that year have robbed him of fees for playing at funerals.

Catalan cellist, conductor, composer and humanitarian Pablo/
Pau Casals, who managed, through his fervent devotion and
magnetic performances, to popularise the cello suites ...

Two gentlemen to whom I should really pay royalties for
use of their material in this book: Johann Nikolaus Forkel
(1749–1818), whose marvellously appreciative and informative
biography of Bach – the first to be written – appeared in 1802.

And Carl Philipp Emanuel Bach (1714–88), who supplied
Forkel with much of his information, and wrote there and
elsewhere about his father with all due deference. (And was a
major, albeit utterly different, composer in his own right, his
music and writings having a strong influence on
Haydn, Mozart, even Beethoven.)

PART 2

The Genesis of the Suites

According to the great humanitarian, theologist, organist and Bach scholar Albert Schweitzer, Bach 'answered ALL the questions brought up by his students'. Lucky students, is all I can say. Would that he could visit us now, if only for a few hours, in order to enlighten us; but given that that is rather unlikely, all we can do is look at all the many doubts, uncertainties and queries revolving around the suites, and get as close as possible to answers – which, I have to warn you, will not always be very close. Oh well – we can but try. Here goes:

WHY . . .
. . . did Bach write the suites?

What could have prompted Bach to write for unaccompanied cello? Annoyingly, there is all too much that we shall (probably) never know about this. There was already quite a bit of music for unaccompanied cello in existence, by composers such as Giuseppe Colombi (1635–94) – his Chiacona for 'basso solo' (presumably a close relative, at least, of the cello) – and Domenico Gabrielli (1659–90) – his famous Ricercari. As the names imply, however, the phenomenon seems to have been confined exclusively to Italy, and it is unlikely that Bach, who was never to venture beyond his own small corner of eastern Germany, would have known, or even known of, these works. (He did know, and actually transcribed, some of the music of Vivaldi, who by the time Bach wrote the suites had already embarked on his series of cello concertos – twenty-seven or twenty-eight at the last count; but Bach was presumably unaware of these works, since they were not published at this time. Incidentally, Bach omitted, as far as we're aware, to write a single cello concerto himself – frustrating.) So why did Bach consider the cello a suitable instrument for unaccompanied music? He wrote no 'continuo' (i.e. accompanied) sonatas – a far more common genre – for us cellists; only these suites for a lonely cello, as well as many wonderful orchestral parts, including several 'obbligato' accompaniments to vocal arias.

Although there seems to have been no precedent in German-speaking countries for unaccompanied cello works, there were quite a few such pieces for solo violin. Apart from the one that is most famous today, the unaccompanied Passacaglia that concludes the celebrated series of 'Mystery' sonatas (with continuo, aside from that movement) by Heinrich Biber (1644–1704), there were compositions for solo violin by several other Germanic composers. As a young man in Weimar Bach may well have known a violinist/composer called Johann Paul von Westhoff, who is said to have been the first to publish music for unaccompanied violin. Even earlier was Thomas Baltzar, who had been born in Bach's area, in the city of Lübeck, in 1631. He seems, in fact, to have specialised in dazzling people with his works for the unaccompanied instrument, receiving a five-star review from Pepys' nearest rival diarist, John Evelyn, after the latter heard him playing in London on 4 March 1656:

> so perfect & skillful as there was nothing so crosse & perplex . . . In Summ, he plaid on that single Instrument a full Consort.

So there were at least models for Bach's famous violin sonatas and partitas; and Bach's own manuscript of these works describes them as 'Libro 1', leaving open the distinct possibility that he may have thought of the cello suites as the second book of a two-part musical tome. (It's also possible, however, that the six sonatas for violin and keyboard were supposed to comprise 'Libro 2'.) But whether or not conceived as a vast whole, the sets for solo violin and cello are very separate, the violin sonatas – as opposed to partitas – in particular far more densely written, with their complex fugues. The partitas are also markedly different from the cello suites, in terms both of string writing and of form. I have often wondered what the distinction is between a partita and a suite, since both are more-or-less large-scale compositions comprising several dance movements. In the case of these particular works, at any rate, I believe that the difference is that the violin partitas are freer in design than the cello suites. Only the third Partita opens with a Prelude; and to the second, the D minor, Bach appends the mighty Chaconne. The suites, in contrast, are in fixed six-movement form, each beginning with a Prelude; only the two-dance sets that make up the fifth movement vary in genre, those of the first two suites being Minuets, those of suites 3 and 4 Bourrées, 5 and 6 Gavottes.

So there are formal and technical differences between the violin and cello works; but there is also a basic difference in atmosphere. Bach was apparently an excellent violinist, at least until his later years (and also an accomplished violist, like so many great composers: Haydn, Mozart, Beethoven, Mendelssohn, Dvořák, Hindemith, Bridge and Britten, among others); but there is no evidence that he played the cello. The solo violin works make full use of four-note chords and contrapuntal textures in a way that Bach does not attempt with the cello, the result being that the cello suites seem to be somehow more intimate, conceived not as concert pieces (or teaching pieces, as Bach's contemporaries seem largely to have considered the violin works), but more as meditations.

On the other hand, it's also true that the writing for cello is perfectly suited to the innate qualities of the instrument – as much as if not more so than in any subsequent compositions. So who, if anybody, was advising Bach?

For WHOM . . .
. . . might the suites have been written?

Well, it *is* possible, even though undocumented, that Bach played the cello himself. Curiously, in one of the few pictures dating from Bach's lifetime that was at one point believed to portray the great man, a family group depicting a father

and three sons, 'Bach' is holding a cello (albeit a small one –
perhaps a violoncello piccolo); but since the portrait seems
unlikely in the end to be of the man himself, that is probably
a red herring.

In Weimar Bach had in his orchestra two cellists (and only
three violinists, not including Bach himself), so it is certainly
possible that one of them may have given him the idea for the
suites. The two most likely candidates, however, are two men
who worked with Bach in Köthen: first would be the famous
gamba player Christian Ferdinand Abel, for whose daughter
Bach stood as godfather. (Abel's son was much later to found
the famous Bach–Abel concerts in London with Bach's
youngest son, Johann Christian.) The main problem with
this theory is that it would necessitate Abel senior having
doubled as a cellist – for which there is no real evidence. It is
true that he is in some modern sources described as a cellist
(and even violinist) as well as gamba player; this is probably,
however, because he played the 'violoncello piccolo', which
is a very different instrument from the real cello – in some
ways more like a gamba than a cello. The portrait mentioned
above, of the gentleman holding a violoncello piccolo, may
well in fact be Abel with three of his children. The other
obvious candidate would be the cellist of Bach's *Kapelle* at
Köthen, Bernhard Lienecke, about whom we know very little. (Although, in an intriguing morsel of trivia, we do know
that he stood as godfather at a christening in Köthen in Sep-
tember 1721; two of the other godparents on this occasion
were Bach and Anna Magdalena – the first time their names
are listed next to each other.)

Or perhaps it was just that Bach, with his restless curiosity, became aware of the possibilities of this emerging instrument, the cello, and wanted to write for it. Again – we shall never know for certain.

For WHAT . . .

. . . instrument were the suites intended?

Well – cello, presumably; but alas, it isn't quite as simple as that. (It rarely is in this story.) For a start, the mainstream cellos that Bach would have known – now thought of as baroque cellos – were markedly dissimilar to our modern instruments: the neck and fingerboard were shorter, the strings made of other materials, the overall set-up different. But, more confusingly, the term 'violoncello'* was loosely used at that time; in addition to the baroque cello, it covered a variety of other, related instruments. We are used to seeing today's players of the baroque cello holding it between their knees, without the modern 'spike', or 'endpin'†; but some of

---

* The formal name one should really use when referring to our wonderful instrument; when I was growing up, people often used an apostrophe before the word 'cello', to indicate that something was missing. Nowadays even that abject little floating comma has gone missing.

† Cello legend maintains – probably unfairly – that the endpin was first adopted by the Belgian cellist François-Adrien Servais (1807–66), when his portly figure made it increasingly difficult for him to hold the cello between his knees. The endpin was then popularised by the first well-known female cellist, Lisa Cristiani (1827–53), who found that it enabled her to play while wearing the skirts of that era without having to resort to playing 'side-saddle' – as most female players did at the time.

these other instruments were placed on a cushioned chair, or held on the shoulder (must have been uncomfortable, even if they were smaller than normal cellos). There were several of these now mostly obsolete animals around at the time: the aforementioned violoncello piccolo (as implied, a small cello), for which Bach wrote quite a few parts in cantatas; the violoncello da braccia – *braccia* meaning 'arm', as opposed to *gamba*, meaning 'leg' (as in the viola da gamba); the viola da spalla (or violoncello da spalla), *spalla* meaning 'shoulder'; the viola pomposa; etc. Further muddying the waters, some of the names may have been interchangeable: for instance, both the violoncello da braccia and the violoncello da spalla may in fact have been the same instrument as a violoncello piccolo.

In three of the four eighteenth-century copies of the Bach suites, they are unequivocally described as being for cello; but in what is probably the earliest copy, by Johann Peter Kellner (1705–72), the title page announces 'Sechs suonaten pour le viola de basso'. However, since he gets the title wrong and can't even stick to one language, perhaps one can discount his evidence. (To be fair, Kellner's description of the suites as 'sonatas' – which would not as a rule contain dances – was a common error; even C. P. E. Bach made the same mistake.) Anyway, since the first four suites are not only written for the normal range of the cello, but exploit the sonic potential of the instrument (bar any special effects, such as pizzicato) to its fullest and most perfect extent, it feels like a pretty safe bet to assume that they were written for the (baroque) cello as we know and love it – even if Bach might not have objected to the suites being played on those other instruments. Thereafter, things appear to become a little more complicated – but only at first glance. The fifth suite calls for 'scordatura', i.e. the retuning of a string – in this case the top string, the A, being tuned down to a G. (This means that in most copies, all the notes that are to be played on what was the A string, but is now an upper G string, are notated a tone higher than they sound, in order to help the cellist to put his or her fingers in the right place.) The practice of scordatura wasn't unusual, however – Biber, for instance, uses it as if there were no tomorrow; it can dramatically transform the sonorities of a string instrument. Then we come to the sixth suite, for which Bach specifies a five-string instrument, with an E string a fifth above the A. This could possibly signify that Bach expected it to be played on a violoncello piccolo (which frequently, though not always, featured just such an upper E string), or on one of those other forgotten instruments. On the other hand, though, there certainly were several five-string cellos around; I think it is more likely that it was written for one of those. Proponents of the violoncello piccolo theory for this suite point to the inventory of string instruments left by Bach after his death; they include both a cello and a 'bassettgen', which may well be yet another name for a violoncello piccolo. That was, however, some thirty years after the suites were probably composed (see below), so it doesn't prove much. Furthermore, there's no score by Bach that specifies 'violoncello piccolo' until his Leipzig years, so were he to have had the piccolo in mind for the sixth suite, that would imply that it was composed somewhat later than the other suites. As it is, for those of us cellists not enamoured of the sound of a five-string cello, or unable to get hold of one, we just struggle along with our four strings, going high up the A string where necessary. I can't say it's easy – but it's eminently possible; and at least we have an excuse for playing out of tune ...

Anyway, the whole argument would probably have seemed futile to Bach, who seems to have been happy to arrange his works for any instrumental combination that was practical.

This is supposedly a violoncello with five strings; personally, I feel that the player – said to be Francesco Alborea, also known as 'Franciscello', the earliest superstar cellist – should concentrate more on how he's going to make a nice sound with a playing position like that and less on looking into the camera.

And then there's the bow: on whichever instrument Bach's contemporaries played, the bow would have been very different from the one used by today's 'modern' players. The baroque bow was more curved than later ones, which gradually (via the 'classical' bow) evolved into today's flatter contour. It would also have been lighter, and the two ends (the 'heel' – commonly known, for some reason, as the 'frog' – and the 'point') would have looked quite dissimilar to their modern counterparts. These disparities mean that early bows are pretty far removed, both in appearance and in feel, from those we know and love today; and consequently they are employed in a very different way. Theories about how bows were used in Bach's time seem to be changing all the time – both concerning how they might have been held, and which bowings would have constituted the norm. For instance, conventional wisdom had us believe for many years that in baroque music all supposedly heavier notes – including practically all the first beats of bars – needed to be played with a down-bow, the lighter ones on an up-bow. However, a few people have now pointed out that the cellists whom Bach knew in Weimar and Köthen may well have held the bow from beneath, in the old gamba style, rather than from above; and it turns out that the rather restrictive down-bow/up-bow, heavy/light rule does not apply to cellists using the 'underhand' technique. (This development pleases me: I've always felt that the only natural way to begin both the third and fourth suites was with an up-bow – and have been criticised for it, especially by certain students. Now I can thumb my generously proportioned nose at such jibes. Ha.) On the other hand – or rather, on the same, right hand – some differences between baroque and modern bows remain important, no matter how Bach's cellists might have held the former. Such differences include the contrast between the baroque bow's predilection for on-the-string bowing, albeit frequently punctuated by flights into the air in order to return to the heel, and the modern bow's tendency to jump away from the string at a moment's notice to produce a staccato articulation. Here the arguments about what is more appropriate for the Bach suites continue to rage, the extreme proponents of modern-type bowing declaring that they no more want to go back in time in terms of musical technique than they do with hygiene (i.e. washing perhaps once a week, and being beset with lice), the 'historically in-formed' obsessives declaring that there is no way to under-stand Bach's music without fully recreating the performance practices of his day. (For what it's worth, I stand somewhere in the middle – fascinated by what I know of baroque bowing conventions, but on the other hand glad of the freedom for my bow to dance its way into the ether when it feels like doing so. Regarding that behaviour of my bow in some movements, I can only fall back on Haydn's answer to those who criti-cised him for writing such cheerful religious music: when he thought of God's mercy, he explained, 'I could not suppress my joy, but gave vent to my happy spirits.' Exactly how my bow feels in, for instance, some of the Courantes and Gigues.)

A 'baroque'-type bow (actually made in the
late twentieth century).

A 'classical' bow.

A 'modern' bow (dating from the early 1800s). All these bows
are from my collection.

Here we have a lady using an underhand bow-hold, with a
gentleman looking on approvingly (though it's hard to tell
whether it's actually the bow-hold of which he approves . . .).

And here we have another gentleman with a (rather odd) over-hand bow-hold, looking thoroughly pleased with himself – as well he might: he is Giacobbe Basevi detto il Cervetto, no less, an Italian/English/Jewish cellist and composer who was born in 1680 and died in 1783 – at the age of 102.

WHEN ...

... were the suites written?

Given the lack of an original manuscript, it is impossible to date the cello suites exactly. It has always been assumed that they were written during the Köthen years, in the course of which Bach produced so much of his instrumental music; but one cannot rule out the possibility of them having been conceived, at least, during the Weimar period. It is also fairly likely that they were revisited later in Leipzig; Bach frequently revised his works, or in some cases made new versions of them. Even though the earliest surviving copy probably dates from as late as 1726, we can surmise that the suites had probably been composed, at least in their first version, by the time Bach left Köthen. His own manuscript of the works for solo violin, specifying them as 'Book 1', is dated 1720; in the much later volume that contains Anna Magdalena's copy of the cello suites, they follow straight on from her copy of the violin sonatas and partitas, and are specifically labelled as 'Part 2'. Therefore, we can rather guardedly accept that both sets of masterpieces were probably conceived and written at roughly the same time. On the other hand, it is just possible (see above) that Bach intended the sixth suite to be played on the aforementioned violoncello piccolo – or even a viola pomposa, an instrument that was probably not even in existence until around 1725. So, questions remain – what a surprise!

Anyway, as a musician I feel that the precise date really doesn't matter that much, other than to historians. What *does* matter to us players, however, is the reliability of the several early sources available to us; and oy vey – that is a veritable can of musical worms . . .

WHICH . . .

. . . of those sources can we trust to have faithfully reproduced Bach's original?

Hmm . . . are you sitting comfortably? Assuming that you are, let's begin by listing the ones we have:

Generally referred to as *Manuscript A* is the copy made by Anna Magdalena Bach and dated (through the paper used) to some time between 1727 and 1731. It formed part of the collection of a violinist named Herr Schwanberger (good name); it's likely that he commissioned – i.e. paid for – the copy. This manuscript was originally bound together with a copy of the solo violin sonatas and partitas, also in Anna Magdalena's hand. It is on the title page of this source that a note in Herr Schwanberger's writing describes the violin works as 'Pars 1', the cello ones as 'Pars 2'; this same page also tells us that the music is 'composée par S. J. S. Bach' and 'écrite par Madame Bachen son Epouse'.

Another copy, known as *Manuscript B* but thought to have been made earlier than A, is in the hand of Johann Peter Kellner, the organist (and possibly something of a violinist, but that's uncertain) mentioned above. Kellner knew Bach, and may have studied with him at one point. Like Anna Magdalena, he copied the solo violin works as well, his version of them being dated 3 July 1726; it would seem that the cello works were written out around the same time.

Next comes a composite manuscript, known to its intimate friends as *Manuscript C*, the first part prepared by a horn player named Johann Nikolaus Schober (*c.*1721–1807), the second (the new scribe taking over in the middle of a bar – curious) by that most widely employed of copyists, Anonymous. This version probably (how often that dreaded word, along with its boon companions 'maybe', 'presumably' and 'possibly', occurs within this history) dates from the 1760s – i.e. some years after Bach's death. Schober worked at the Prussian court in Berlin alongside C. P. E. Bach, so we can fairly safely assume that he was copying from a source owned by the latter (see below). Manuscript C was at one point owned by another organist, Johann Christian Westphal (1773–1829), whose father, a music-dealer, had known C. P. E. Bach in Hamburg, where C. P. E. spent his last twenty years.

Also copied by Anonymous – but a different member of the tribe – *Manuscript D* hails from Hamburg and dates from the late years of the eighteenth century. It closely resembles Manuscript C, and was probably (aargh) commissioned by C. P. E.'s daughter, Anna Karoline Philippina Bach (1747–1804).

So there we have the four earliest surviving copies of the suites. Since Manuscripts C and D were created during the second half of the eighteenth century rather than during Bach's lifetime, it's tempting to dismiss them as less relevant; but as it turns out, they have as good a claim as manuscripts A and B to be faithful reproductions of Bach's original – maybe . . .

Then we have several other versions to consider:

Bach's original manuscript – or manuscripts? LOST.

A copy owned by C. P. E. Bach, from which Manuscripts C and D must (almost certainly) have been copied. LOST.

An autograph of the transcription made by Bach of the fifth suite, transposed into G minor, for lute (a.k.a. the third lute suite). One might think that this would simplify things, but it turns out that, interesting though it is to see how Bach both harmonises and embellishes the music, in the matter of articulation (which constitutes the major difference between the sources) it complicates matters still further. Of course . . .

Finally, there is in addition the beautiful manuscript, in J. S.'s own magisterial hand, of the violin solo sonatas and partitas, which one has to examine for comparison during the search to discover what Bach might actually have written into the manuscript(s) of the cello suites.

And, not that it's much use (except to scholars seeking to understand how Bach was performed in the early nineteenth century), there's also the heavily edited first edition of the suites prepared by a French cellist called Louis-Pierre

Norblin; this did not appear until 1824 – so around a hundred years after their composition. Norblin had somehow heard about the suites; perhaps he'd read Forkel's biography of Bach, in which they are described as being of equal value to the violin works. In a preface to his edition, Norblin congratulates himself on having found the manuscript, after a long search in Germany; however, it seems pretty certain that the manuscript he'd found was either the one owned by C. P. E. (in which case there is a small chance that it was the – an – autograph) or manuscript C or D. Anyway, Monsieur Norblin distorts the music with his addition of masses of tempo indications, slurs and dynamics which, even if some of them may make a certain musical sense, are just not necessary; we players need to get closer to Bach's original, not further away from it – and then make our musical decisions for ourselves. He doesn't even get the title right, designating them as 'Six Sonates ou Etudes pour le Violoncello Solo'. Studies indeed . . .

'Anyway,' I hear you say, 'what's the problem? You lucky cellists have four early sources; you just read them all, decide which suits you best – and hey presto, you have a valid reading of the suites.' Well, yes and no; but mostly no. When one plays music as great as this, attention to each and every detail is what separates a true, speaking performance from an average, run-of-the-mill one; divining and following the composer's intentions – not necessarily literally, but absolutely faithfully, in what one feels to be the spirit and language of the music – is the chief duty of the interpreter. And that is an exact science, not a matter for blind guesswork. In order to provide convincing interpretations, we need to be convinced.

'Ah, but are a few disparities that important?' I hear you continue (my imagination has good hearing). Well – yes, they are. Actually, strange to say, it's not really the different notes that matter the most here. There is certainly a wide range of contradictory readings of various notes or chords to be found, but in most cases these are either alternative viable possibilities or obvious errors that can be quite easily corrected. Of course, there is much room for discussion, but nothing (I'd say) that lies at the true heart of interpretation. For example, here is the ending of a bar from the Prelude to the first suite, where Anna Magdalena and Kellner have the following:

whereas sources C and D have this:

i.e. Anna Magdalena thinks that these two beats are composed of the notes A, C sharp, E, G, A, C sharp, D, C sharp, while sources C and D would have us play A, C sharp, E, F sharp, G, A, B flat, C sharp. Both look as if they were very deliberately written; either is credible – one just has to choose. More of a bumper issue is a chord in the penultimate bar of the Sarabande of the sixth suite. This, as far as I can see, is the only time where all four sources have different notes. (All the Fs here are F sharps, as per the key signature.) Anna Magdalena has:

i.e. G in the bass; Kellner says it's G sharp:

No, you're both wrong, says source C:

It's A, obviously.

Ha! I can trump that, crows source D:

It's A, but with an F sharp beneath it.

So – there are decisions to be made; but I wouldn't say that they deeply affect the meaning of the music. Nor do the important discrepancies lie in tempo indications – Anna Magdalena's version has none, the others very few; or dynamics – as with much baroque music, these are sparse (again, particularly in Anna Magdalena's copy). The greatest problem by far, as I've mentioned, lies in the specified articulation, the (many) slurs indicating which notes should be played within one bow-stroke. Here again, you might be entitled to be dubious. 'Surely bowings don't really make *that* much difference?' Well, yes – unfortunately they do. IfIwereto writelikethis – orli keth is – you mightbeslightly puzzled; and that's the effect of misplaced slurs in performance. A very important part of the interpreter's task in this music – in any music – is to decide which notes belong together and which should be separated; which are strong, which weak. Changing the bow also allows the music/the bow to breathe in the right place – essential. Without that, one gets an effect like this of a narrative going on and on lacking punctuation one doesn't really want that it quickly becomes incomprehensible music has its commas its semicolons its full colons its full stops it even has inverted commas phew.

The trouble is that the intention behind misplaced slurs can be difficult to decipher, to put it mildly. Let's look at the manuscripts and see wherein the problem lies, taking as a starting point the first two lines of perhaps the most famous movement of all, the Prelude of the first suite, in G major. Here's Anna Magdalena's version:

Here's Kellner's:

Now Manuscript C:

Then there's Manuscript D:

And here (not that it matters much, but it sets the tone for nearly a hundred years of performances) is the first edition:

True, all the notes are the same – but as for the articulation markings . . .

This opening comprises a serene arpeggiated figure rising over three strings. In the first bar the notes are the principal ones of the home key, G major: G, D, B. G is the 'tonic'; D is the fifth, or 'dominant'; and B is the third, or 'mediant'. The fourth note to be heard, A, is the only one not to belong to the home 'triad' of G major – meaning that it would sound (mildly) discordant if played at the same time as the other three. During the second beat we get the B and the D repeated twice, this time with the high B played first, so going down rather than up. The third and fourth beats are a replica of the first two. Rhythmically, the bar consists of a repeated pattern of sixteen notes, all of equal duration, called semiquavers – or sixteenth notes, depending on whether you speak English or American. (From now on, I'll use the English terms – for the UK edition, anyway. Actually, in rehearsal I tend to use the American version – it's so much more logical, if arguably less quaintly charming.) Despite all the words I have just employed in order to describe these four beats, they are in fact extremely simple, as are the subsequent three bars – or rather, they should be; but the bewildering disparities between these copies are enough to cause conscientious players deep grief and bewilderment. Look at them! (The disparities, not the players.)

Anna Magdalena marks the slurs in the first bar over the B and A – the two notes that really *don't* belong together. Furthermore, although the basic musical pattern continues unchanged in shape (even if the notes are different) for the next three bars, she never repeats that slur over the third and fourth notes of said pattern. In fact, her slurs dance around all over the place (as they do in her copy of the solo violin works, the inaccuracies particularly striking when one compares her version with her husband's well-nigh perfect manuscript). Hmm . . . maybe she was distracted by the plethora of stepchildren and children? Or perhaps she'd been swigging from the beer that formed part of Bach's salary, or the wine or brandy so close to his heart? (To digress just slightly: apparently one of the chief reasons that people of the time imbibed so freely was that alcohol protected them from the bacteria present in the water they drank. That was their story, anyway.)

At any rate, I think we can declare with some certitude that Anna Magdalena makes a mistake in the very first bar of the very first suite. Bach's music is always dictated by a divine logic; there's nothing random. As Forkel observed:

> With him, every transition was required to have a connection with the preceding idea and to appear to be a necessary consequence of it. He knew not, or rather he disdained, those sudden sallies by which many composers attempt to surprise their listeners.

And playing the first bar the way Anna Magdalena wrote it would sound too much like a sudden sally in a Leipzig alley, even if there's nothing preceding it.

Hmm . . . it hardly augurs well for the reliability of the whole manuscript. (Nor is one's confidence in her attention to detail boosted later when she gives the title of 'Courante' to the Allemande of the fifth suite.)

Now look at Mr Kellner's version. (Sorry: do stop me if I'm being boring.) He at least has the initial slur over the first three notes – but it also appears to cover the fourth (which could be valid, although it seems to me odd to group the 'foreign' note, A, with the triad). But then, looking further, his slurs also seem to develop minds of their own, changing shape every bar; it's impossible to tell how many notes they're supposed to cover. Again, logic and natural musicality suggest that the slurs should be the same in all of the first four bars; there's just no reason for them to differ.

At least Manuscript C is consistent, thank goodness, the first three notes of each group slurred each time; but Manuscript D, after a promising start, also goes mad, with the slur starting to creep over the fourth note, and with an incomprehensible slur over the second beat of bar 3. What was in the stuff they drank in those days? Meanwhile, the first edition has firmly decided that the first slur is supposed to cover the four notes of the group, not just three. As I say, this is possible, even though I strongly doubt whether it's correct; and it's certainly preferable to later editions, in which the first bars contained just two slurs, each covering eight notes. This rather slimy bowing became standard for many years, in fact, and made it well-nigh impossible for the passage to speak or dance.

Here, complete with utterly redundant crescendo, is the Hugo Becker edition – the first incarnation in which I, and countless other cellists, encountered the suites:

Violoncello.

So – the first bar of the first of the suites is already causing us heartache and sleepless nights; and there are thirty-one more bars in this Prelude, and then thirty-five or forty-one more complete movements (depending on whether you count the double movements as one or two) to go. Now maybe you can begin to understand why it is that if you see someone in the street looking pale and gaunt, muttering to themselves, it is quite likely to be a cellist who has been studying the Bach suites. Oh well – there are rewards too …

But WHY are there such differences between the earliest sources? Well, there are two distinct – at times warring – schools of thought on this issue: some scholars claim that the massive variants are a result of the four copies stemming from at least two different versions in Bach's hand; while other experts tut-tut and say that this is impossible, that they were all definitely taken from the same one manuscript – pointing as (quite convincing) evidence to the mistakes that all four copies have in common, errors that Bach would surely not have made twice in different autographs. Proponents of the two points of view are often at each other's throats (in print, anyway). It can be quite amusing to witness – as can many spats among historians, musical and otherwise. I am a member of various societies devoted to composers – partly because I'm interested in those composers, and partly because I find it so funny to read such things as, for instance, Professor Y's triumphant assertion that Professor Z is quite wrong to say that Liszt arrived in Bologna on 30 October, because here is a restaurant bill from a Bologna restaurant dated 28 October. The next newsletter is then likely to contain a furious letter from Professor Z, pointing out that the 28 October bill – as all the world (except Professor Y, evidently) knows – actually dates from the previous year, when Liszt was between Modena and Imola and stopped off for lunch in Bologna between 1 and 3 p.m.; with all due respect (i.e. very little), Professor Z suggests that Professor Y should have done her homework, and perhaps had her eyesight checked, before making such preposterous allegations. And so on . . .

How amazed the composers themselves would have been to witness the fights that occur nowadays over the trivia of their lives; though not as amazed, I think it's fair to say, as aristocratic musical patrons (such as the Margrave of Brandenburg, or Prince Leopold of Köthen, in Bach's case) would have been to discover that they are now remembered solely for their connection with a mere employee – a humble musician at that. Probably most astonished of all, however, would have been the composers' copyists and other helpers, to know that *their* lives and work (Bach's assistants in particular) are now the object of minute scrutiny, with multiple research foundations and laboratories devoted to studying their handwriting, the paper and ink they used at different times, etc. Such attention might seem like madness, in fact . . .

... but it's exactly what we have to give to the four copyists involved here, in order to get a little closer to the truth about the suites.

First, Anna Magdalena: as far as we know, she was a very fine singer (employed as such in Leipzig at a musician's salary second only to that of her husband), though almost certainly less advanced as a keyboard player; she was evidently much involved with various musical activities of her husband, giving regular concerts with him as well as copying out many of his pieces. There is no record, however, of her ever having played a string instrument. Bach himself, in addition to all his other accomplishments, was – as already mentioned – an excellent violinist; C. P. E. recalled that until his old age, Bach played the violin 'cleanly and powerfully'. Bach's slurs, therefore – such as those in the solo violin works – are the markings of a string player, presumably indicating bowings rather than just phrasing. (When it comes to slurs, those in music for violin and for cello will in general be pretty identical. Sometimes, it is true, at a point where it will feel comfortable for a violinist to play a down-bow, it will feel more appropriate to the cellist to use an up-bow, or vice versa; but since there are no down-bow or up-bow indications in the suites, that detail need not concern us here.) Some composers who were not practising string players – Debussy, to take one random example – mark slurs that are impossible to contain within one bow-stroke; they are there to indicate the shape or character of the phrase, not precise execution. That does not seem to be the case with Bach, whose markings are generally thoroughly practical; but

Anna Magdalena, as a non-string player, evidently did not approach that aspect of her copies with as much care as her husband. Much though she must have revered Herr Bach's work (how could she not?), she almost certainly had no idea of the importance every stroke of her pen would have for future musicians. How/why could/should she? Besides, she was probably in a rush.

As for Kellner, he was primarily an organist; he may also have dabbled in violin-playing, but not significantly. It is surmised that he copied out both the solo violin works and the cello suites with a view to arranging them for himself to play on the organ, especially since they are contained within a large volume of pieces containing mostly keyboard music. (Similarly, Bach himself was reported to have played his own solo violin works on the clavichord, and would also presumably have performed the organ version of the first movement of the E major partita, which he incorporated within the opening Sinfonia of his cantata BWV 29.) This would explain why Kellner makes no mention of the fifth string in the sixth suite and why in the fifth, he tries to correct the scordatura writing and notate the upper tones as they are supposed to sound. (We know that he was writing from a copy containing the scordatura notation but attempting to transpose to real pitch, because he makes so many mistakes.) We can't be certain, however (just for a change), that this explains the huge volume of differences between Kellner's versions and the others. In fact, there are several mysteries hovering around his copies of both sets of string works. Why, for instance, does he leave out the entire

first partita for violin (the B minor) as well as several movements of the other two partitas, and large chunks of some
of the movements that he did copy – in particular the Chaconne, of which some seventy bars have gone astray? When
it comes to the cello suites, he omits the timeless, haunting
Sarabande from the fifth suite, as well as all but the opening few bars of the Gigue of that suite. One theory that has
been posited is that he was working in both cases from an
earlier, incomplete copy of the music. It's almost impossible
to imagine the fifth suite (the world, in fact) without that
Sarabande; but it is *conceivable*, I suppose, that Bach, un-
sure of what to write as the central movement, temporarily
omitted the Sarabande, and jumped to the Gavottes, as well
as leaving the final movement, the Gigue, unfinished on a
draft copy – and that Kellner somehow got hold of this version. Hmm . . . as Sherlock Holmes advises us: 'When you
have eliminated the impossible, whatever remains, *however
improbable*, must be the truth.' Unarguable, but here there
are also other possibilities. This 'unfinished draft' idea just
doesn't ring true: why would everything else in the suites
be complete other than these two movements? Another hy-
pothesis – one that to me, at least, seems far more likely – is
that Kellner was only interested in those movements that he
felt would work as organ pieces. Neither this Sarabande –
the only movement with very few added harmonies in the
lute version – nor the Gigue contain any chords or double-
stopping, only single notes; so he may have given up on
them as useless. (This doesn't explain why he left a truncated version of the Chaconne; but I leave it to those writing

about the violin works to explain that one away.) Anyway, it shows, I feel, that his version is not to be trusted implicitly as a faithful transcription of the master's final thoughts on the suites – even though he does seem, at least, to have corrected a few wrong notes found in the other three sources. I suspect, finally, that one must treat Kellner's version with just as much caution as Anna Magdalena's; or perhaps even more. In his defence, however, it should be acknowledged that Kellner took the trouble to write out a huge quantity of Bach's music, including some pieces that would otherwise have been lost. For that, and for the fact that he evidently appreciated the genius of Bach when few did, we should show him some gratitude and respect – and defend him from the many scholars who have given him a thoroughly rough ride.

And so to Manuscripts C and D: I think we can deal with them together because, though by no means identical, they are similar enough for us to assume that they were copied from the same source; or perhaps D is a copy of C. But what was the source for C? It's an important question. Looking at these two versions in the past, and knowing that they came into existence well after Bach's death, I tended to overlook them – partly, somehow, because the bowings are *too* sensible and pragmatic; I assumed that they were the work of a cellist, or cellists, who wanted to perform the suites and so added their own bowings. But perhaps – dreaded thought – I was wrong . . .

And that, I'm afraid, necessitates another digression:

C. P. E. Bach's copy

It seems fairly clear, given the provenance of Manuscripts C and D, that they would have originated from the version that we know C. P. E. Bach left in his estate (and which has since disappeared – naturally). So who was the source of that source? It appears unlikely that it was J. S. himself, since in the catalogue of C. P. E.'s collection of his father's music it is stated clearly that both the two previous entries, *The Art of Fugue* and the 15 Inventions and Sinfonias, are in Bach's hand ('in origineller Handschrift'), whereas the entry for the suites tells us merely that it was written out ('geschriebene') and bound ('eingebunden'). Not a hundred per cent proof, true; but that does seem to imply quite strongly that it's not an original autograph.

Die Kunst der Fuge in origineller Handschrift.
15 Inventionen und 15 Sinfonien fürs Clavier, in origineller Handschrift. Eingebunden.
6 geschriebene Suiten fürs Violoncell ohne Baß. Eingebunden.
6 Präludien für Anfänger auf dem Clavier.

If not by Bach himself, however, the copy might instead – perhaps? – have been made by a gentleman named Johann Christoph Altnickol (1719–59). This is conjecture, with no evidence attached; however, it is possible. Altnickol did write out a lot of Bach's music; and if it was indeed he who created

C. P. E.'s manuscript of the suites – then this is serious! Altnickol came to Leipzig in 1744 and, having started out as a student of Bach's, seems to have become progressively closer to the Bach family – coming as close as one could get, in fact, by marrying Bach's daughter Elisabeth Juliane Friederica in 1749. Their first son was born nine months later, and was christened Johann Sebastian; alas, he died in infancy – unlike Carl Philipp Emanuel's son Johann Sebastian Bach (1748–78), who became a successful artist. Forkel even tells us that Bach on his deathbed dictated his last work, the Chorale Prelude 'Vor deinen Thron' – actually a revision of an earlier chorale – to Altnickol; although doubts have been cast on the accuracy of this legend, Forkel would not have recorded it unless he'd had it from a reliable source – C. P. E.? After his father-in-law's death, Altnickol and his wife may have assumed partial responsibility for Bach's apparently mentally challenged (but musically talented, of course!) son, Gottfried Heinrich. Altnickol was not merely an expert scribe, evidently trusted by the Bachs (J. S. himself kept Altnickol's copy of *The Well-Tempered Clavier* Book 2 in his possession until his death), but also a composer in his own right, a singer, organist, conductor, violinist – and cellist. He took part, presumably in various capacities, in the house concerts during which Bach gave almost all of his performances outside churches in his last years. Is it even possible that Altnickol might have performed the cello suites during these concerts, having made a copy for this very purpose, with some corrections/additions provided by Bach himself? It's a tempting thought, particularly since Manuscripts C and D are more performer-friendly than either of the earlier sources; in a potential parallel, Altnickol's copy of the six sonatas for violin and keyboard is generally accepted as the final version of those works. And he wrote so beautifully.

Altnickol's manuscript, in his calligraphy-worthy handwriting, of a Sanctus of his own composition.

So we can say of this idea that it's at least imaginable, and also that it would somehow make sense; but yet again, of one thing we can be fairly certain – that we shall never be certain. And there are so many other possibilities: for instance, C. P. E. Bach's copy could just as easily have been the work of the same anonymous scribe who entered a fair copy of 'Vor deinen Thron' into a volume of Bach's organ chorales, probably shortly after Bach's death; this copyist, whose work first appears around 1742, is believed to have worked later for C. P. E. in Berlin, so that gives him a fighting chance with the bookies. Then there are the two unknown copyists who produced a manuscript of Bach's sonatas for violin and keyboard that was also in C. P. E.'s possession; and so on. The trouble is that there are eighteenth-century copies of Bach's music in well over a hundred different hands. But I do like the Altnickol idea – keeping it in the family, as it were . . .

In the end – who knows?

Nobody. All the witnesses seem to be dead – highly suspicious. A cover-up, say I.

* * *

At any rate, I think that, amidst all the uncertainty, this does suggest that both performers and historians should lavish as much attention on Manuscripts C and D as they do the two earlier sources. As well as containing eminently practical bowings, C and D offer us many more dynamic markings than do either Anna Magdalena or Kellner, as well as frequent staccato indications, almost entirely lacking in the first two sources; and in addition – interestingly – some very attractive ornamentation. Could these embellishments be the work of Bach? As my friend John Butt pointed out in his wonderfully helpful notes for this book, Bach frequently inserted extra ornaments into students' copies of his own work – as John puts it, 'For Bach, less is bore'; or as Forkel observes, rather less succinctly: 'I confess that I have often felt both surprise and delight at the means which he employed to make, little by little, the faulty good, the good better, and the better perfect.' Musically, I'd say it was certainly possible that the added ornamentation was Bach's; but of course it could also be the work of a tasteful performer who understood the style of the suites (Altnickol?).

Manuscript C, despite being the work of two scribes, also has the virtue of being the most consistently legible of the four, particularly after Herr Anonymous takes over (although all four manuscripts are picturesque in their various ways). Looking at Bach's glorious autograph of the violin partitas/sonatas, a work of art in itself, I'd say that all the copies of the cello suites come fairly close to it in terms of general bowing patterns – particularly Bach's habit of separating one note within groups of four, which all our suite scribes reproduce to a greater or (slightly) lesser degree. The devil is in the details, which vary to an eye-watering degree. The lute manuscript in Bach's hand (only marginally less beautiful than the violin works) doesn't really help that much, as mentioned earlier. The trouble is that he writes quite differently for lute, so that while this undoubtedly authentic source does answer some questions, it then poses more. Curiously, if a copy of the cello version wins on the basis of proximity to this lute manuscript, it is Kellner's; his version does display some notable similarities, despite that unhelpful omission of the Sarabande and Gigue.

So finally, the million-thaler question: were they all – including the manuscript in C. P. E.'s collection, presuming that it was not an original – copied from the same one manuscript, or from more than one source in Bach's hand? Here the pitchfork battles begin: those in favour of the one-source theory, as I mentioned earlier, point to the errors that all the copies have in common – most of which can be explained away (if a little uncertainly in some instances), but not all. To take just one example – all four manuscripts have a curious rhythmic mistake in common: the upbeat to bar 1 in the Allemande of the fifth suite is written as a semiquaver, which makes perfect sense. The corresponding note, however, the upbeat to the second half of the movement, is written in all the copies as a quaver. It's not just unlikely, but – I'd say – impossible on musical grounds that those two notes are supposed to be of different values. 'Ha!' say the one-source brigade; 'that proves that all four copies stem from one manuscript.' 'Ha yourself!' counter the two-or-more-sources contingent; 'so how do you explain the enormous differences between Anna Magdalena, Kellner and versions C and D? They're so utterly unalike' – continue the multiple-sources army – 'that it is quite impossible that all four can stem from the same foundation.' And both camps growl and snarl and recommend delusion therapy for their opposite numbers. How bemused Bach himself would have been to observe all this. True, he *must* have known how far ahead his music was of any other that he saw or heard (even though he was said to be 'uncommonly modest, tolerant, and very polite' to other musicians); but I've no doubt that in his own eyes he was just a thoroughly hard-working musician, composing (as he used to write on his manuscripts) 'Soli Deo gloria' – 'To the Glory of God Alone' – and would have been baffled by the present near-obsession with his music. Well, as Mel Brooks so wisely put it: 'Immortality is a by-product of good work.'*

Finally, I suppose that the rather uneasy compromise version is that perhaps Bach wrote the suites out only once, but kept adding to and altering that one manuscript (though evidently not to the extent of correcting several mistakes – which is mighty strange). Or that perhaps source A stems (as does B?) from a manuscript in Bach's hand, the others from a lost copy made by Altnickol or another Bach acolyte with additions by the master. And that, I suspect, is as close as we can get. (Luckily, at the time of writing, I have enough hair left to allow me to tear some strands of it without yielding to baldness – unlike, I strongly suspect, Bach himself underneath that wig. A wig, incidentally, which he was known to tear off and throw at his musicians in moments of extreme frustration . . .)

At any rate, it's likely that the copyists of the suites did not have an easy task. If (if!) they were all working from the same autograph, it must have looked more like this:

---

* Herbert Gold, 'Funny is Money', *New York Times*, 30 March 1975.

From autograph of cantata BWV 9.

than this:

The opening of the first of the sonatas for solo violin,
in Bach's fair copy.

And so we come back to the other million-thaler (plus some beer) question: which of the sources is to be trusted most? Well, assuming that those two hypothetical scenarios – either one working manuscript, or one such manuscript and another (or others) with additions in Bach's hand – are the most likely original sources, there's a strong possibility that all four surviving copies have fairly equally direct links to Bach; and so, after all that, we have to decide for ourselves which of the four contenders best represents the master's final thoughts.

Meanwhile, just to add another much-needed layer of complication, even if there *were* a copy in Bach's hand, it might not represent his last word. With some of his works the autograph is superseded by a later version in another hand, but with emendations by Bach; this should probably be seen as the composer's definitive text – even if that does not necessarily make it musically preferable to an earlier one.

It's also quite possible that the reason that there is no fair copy in Bach's hand is that he saw no reason ever to make one. In the absence of any publisher interested in printing them, or a cellist able or willing (so far as we know) to perform them, perhaps he never bothered; the labour would have taken a lot of time and energy. And if one looks at how few obbligato movements for cello – compared to, say, violin or oboe – there are in the Leipzig cantatas, one can hazard a guess that the cellists available to Bach there were not virtuosi, as the Köthen ones seem to have been. (True – there's lots of exciting stuff in Bach's Leipzig works in the continuo department, of which the cello would have formed an important element; but those parts would have been doubled by a keyboard, and usually a violone, thus lessening the responsibility of the cellist.)

As a short postscript to this lengthy disquisition, I have to include a thought about the lack of a fair copy in Bach's hand that was included in a fascinating article about Bach and numbers by the distinguished musicologist Ruth Tatlow.[*]

---

[*] Ruth Tatlow, 'Collections, Bars and Numbers: Analytical Coincidence or Bach's Design?' You can read this online at https://www.bachnetwork.org/ub2/tatlow.pdf. Tatlow is also the author of a book on the subject: *Bach's Numbers: Compositional Proportion and Significance* (Cambridge University Press, 2015).

She points out the importance of perfect mathematical proportions in Bach's music, demonstrating it with some amazing figures relating to his works for violin. For instance, in the first sonata for solo violin, the opening three movements contain 136 bars; the fourth and final movement also contains 136 bars. In the first partita, the first six movements make up a total of 272 bars, exactly twice as many as the last two; furthermore, the sonata has exactly two-thirds as many bars as the partita. Of course, this could be a coincidence – but then, consider the following: the total number of bars in the first two sonatas and partitas combined is exactly twice that of the third sonata and partita. Then, moving on to the six sonatas for violin and keyboard: similarly, those first four sonatas contain exactly twice as many bars as the last two. Not only that, but the total number of bars within the first four works for solo violin – sixteen hundred – is exactly the same as in the equivalent works for violin and keyboard; the same is true of the remaining two works in both sets, each of which contains eight hundred bars in total. Tatlow also points out that this is only true of the final versions of the sets – which are in Bach's hand in the case of the solo violin works, and in Altnickol's for the violin/keyboard works. Other versions of the collections (presuming that Kellner's truncated Chaconne stems from an earlier draft, and including Bach's arrangement of the E major partita for lute) do not display these perfect proportions. So Tatlow concludes that if the cello suites had been written out in fair copy, they would have incorporated minor revisions to ensure that the numbers all added up. In fact, she does detect some of those proportions within the suites, but only if one observes some extremely peculiar repeat markings to be found in Anna Magdalena's copy, at the end of some of the Preludes. Might it be possible to play the Preludes twice? Surely not?* The mind, it boggleth. Curiouser and curiouser . . .

Turning back, with heads spinning, to the manuscript question for a final time . . . ('Phew!' I heard you say. Don't deny it.) We repeat your question: ultimately, does it really matter that we don't have the autograph? Well – yes, it does, in fact. True, we can – we must, in fact – take our pick from the four versions, and decide upon bowings that seem logical and natural, and then allow ourselves the option to change them each time we play the suites. Perhaps this even gives us a certain welcome freedom. It's also true that most composers will accept alternative bowings, if they are (tactfully) suggested by a performer who understands the music. But – dammit: it makes our life harder. Our chief mission as interpreters is to put ourselves into the mind, the soul of the composer; and that Herculean task becomes even more challenging if we're unable to see the evidence. We want, we *need*, to know what Bach really wrote. Alas, in this case, that can never be – unless the (an?) autograph miraculously reappears. One can always hope, I suppose . . .

* My friend, editor extraordinaire Jonathan Del Mar, suggests that Anna Magdalena, having written out so many dance movements (which are almost all repeated), had become so used to putting repeat markings at the end of each movement that she mistakenly added them to some of the Preludes as well. If so, another example of her distracted state . . .

So in the end, our performance choices have to come down to our personal taste and judgement. We look, we detect, we sift, we cogitate – we agonise. I suppose that many Christians must wish that the authors of the four Gospels had consulted a bit further before penning their often contradictory accounts; we cellists feel the same about the suites.

And HOW . . .
. . . did the suites fare during the years after their composition?

Bach's music was not completely forgotten after his death. A few of his works – mostly for keyboard, whether harpsichord or organ – had been published during the composer's lifetime, mostly at his own expense; so they were (somewhat) available, at least. A few unpublished works somehow became known, too. Forkel tells us, in that 1802 biography, that 'for a long series of years the violin solos were universally considered by the greatest performers on the violin to be the best means to make an ambitious student a perfect master of his instrument'. Meanwhile, in late-eighteenth-century Vienna, as mentioned earlier, Mozart was introduced to several of Bach's works by Baron van Swieten, a fanatic for baroque music, who was to prepare the libretti for Haydn's late oratorios, *The Creation* and *The Seasons*. (Incidentally, Forkel's Bach biography is dedicated to the baron – as is Beethoven's first symphony.) Later, Mozart got the chance to hear some more of Bach's choral works in Leipzig. An eyewitness reported:

As soon as the choir had sung a few bars, Mozart started; after a few more he exclaimed: 'What is that?' And now his whole soul seemed to be centred in his ears. When the song was ended, he cried out with delight: 'Now, here is something one can learn from!'

Just a few years earlier, the first-ever review of Beethoven, written when he was eleven years old, has this to say:

He plays chiefly *The Well-Tempered Clavier* of Sebastian Bach, which Herr Neefe [Beethoven's teacher] put into his hands. Whoever knows this collection of preludes and fugues in all the keys – which might almost be called the *non plus ultra* of our art – will know what this means.

So Bach was not forgotten – but his cello suites were. There is no record of a performance for at least a hundred years. It's true that that they might have been played by one of Bach's cellists in Köthen or Leipzig, or later perhaps by one of the anonymous copyists of Manuscripts C or D, or their friends; we have no way of knowing. It's pretty certain, however, that they were not a fixture on concert programmes during the century after they came into being. It was not until Monsieur Norblin published his edition in 1824 – presumably based, directly or indirectly, on C. P. E. Bach's manuscript copy – that they began to be more widely disseminated; this first publication was followed by three more within as many years – two of them, appropriately, in

Leipzig. Then, in 1829, Mendelssohn gave his famous Berlin performance of the *St Matthew Passion*; this gave Bach's reputation a huge boost – even though the work was presented in a somewhat truncated version. In 1831, a further edition of the suites appeared in Leipzig. After that, things went a bit quiet; but by now, the suites were starting to be appreciated – by those who mattered, at least . . .

Schumann and the Suites

Robert Schumann in 1853.

Robert Schumann (1810–56) had always been a Bach fanatic: 'I myself confess daily to this eminent creator and seek to purify and strengthen myself through him.' He was one of the founders of the Bach Gesellschaft, the society that aimed to produce the first complete and scholarly edition of Bach's music, a far-reaching project – the cello suites would not appear until 1879. In 1851, inspired by Mendelssohn's work on the *St Matthew Passion* – Mendelssohn having repeated it in Leipzig, where Schumann was then living, in 1841 – he prepared his own version of the *St John Passion* for a performance in Düsseldorf. In late 1852/early 1853, further stimulated by Mendelssohn's piano accompaniment for the Chaconne, Schumann composed piano accompaniments for Bach's complete works for solo violin. He wrote to the publisher: 'I hope that the harmonic braces [*tragehänder*] which I fastened to them will help bring these treasures up to the surface.' Soon thereafter, he turned his attention to the cello suites, providing them with a piano accompaniment also. On 17 November 1853 (just a few months before his final breakdown and removal to the asylum in which he was, tragically, to spend his last two and a half years), he wrote to a different publisher, Kistner, about them, adding that the suites 'are the most beautiful and important compositions for the cello'. Annoyingly, that publisher refused the offer. Undaunted, Schumann arranged for the first cellist in his Düsseldorf orchestra, Christian Reimers, to play them through: nos. 1–3 on New Year's Eve 1853, 4–6 on New Year's Day 1854.

A few years after Schumann's death, a publisher named Schuberth (sic) showed an interest in the accompaniments. Schumann's widow Clara turned to her friends Brahms and Joachim; alas, their reaction was negative (particularly Brahms'), and thereafter Clara suppressed and probably destroyed her husband's work, along with the Romances for cello and piano that he had written around the same time. To add to the frustration, we know that the suite accompaniments survived for many years in another copy (very possibly with a copy of the Romances as well); Reimers moved to England and thence to Australia, where he regularly performed movements from the suites with Schumann's piano parts. We were fated to be denied them, however: Reimers died on a ship in 1889, on his way back to Europe. It would seem that his body was unceremoniously (or ceremoniously) thrown overboard, along – probably – with his belongings. (Hopefully the fish in those parts enjoyed Schumann's music, at least.) Meanwhile, a certain Dr W. Stade had published the six suites, along with an accompaniment that he claimed he'd based on Schumann's, adding, though, that his was 'correct'; it seems to have been a fake, however. More recently, a copy was found of just the third suite, with an accompanying piano part; this manuscript was dated 1863, written out in the hand of a long-forgotten cellist called Julius Goltermann (unrelated to the more famous cellist Georg Goltermann, with whose études young cellists today are still tortured). Again, J. Goltermann claimed that it was Schumann's accompaniment; perhaps it was – it has been published as such. I can't say that I'm a hundred per cent convinced – but maybe . . .

Anyway, well meaning though Schumann's accompaniments, and several more made over the years, undoubtedly were, they were also completely superfluous. One of the main glories of the suites (and of course the solo violin works as well) lies in their miraculous use of the unaccompanied instrument to create a whole world of sound, with no need for anything else to be added. As Forkel put it, Bach 'has so combined in a single part all the notes required to make the modulation complete that a second part is neither necessary nor possible'. But we should not be harsh on Schumann's attitude; after all, Bach himself had added cornetto, trombones and continuo to Palestrina's Liber V Missarum, as well as setting Pergolesi's Stabat Mater to completely different – German – words.

* * *

So back to the career of the suites in their proper, solo incarnation: before that scholarly 1879 Bach Gesellschaft edition – a turning point in the history of the suites – there had been, as noted earlier, five new editions of the suites. The trouble is that they were all, in their different ways, distortions; they couldn't even get the title right, referring to the suites as either sonatas or études – not a promising start. It does seem as if people misunderstood the true nature of the music. It became quite common as the nineteenth century progressed for cellists to play isolated movements in concerts, with or without piano. (Not everyone was delighted by this trend. In 1886, Hugo Wolf remarked sarcastically, after hearing a concert by Brahms' friend, the cellist Robert Hausmann: 'May a Bach sarabande and bourrée excite visions and the sound of angel voices; may one be a lunatic and find a redeeming world-riddle behind every note from the pen of the great Bach.') It was rare, however, for anyone to play an entire suite. One exception was the German cellist Friedrich Grützmacher

(1832–1903). He is best remembered today – by cellists, at least – for his mind-numbing reworking of Boccherini's lovely, innocent concerto in B flat, which Grützmacher converted into a Victorian mishmash. (Well, that's my view of it, anyway – though admittedly I'm a Boccherini fanatic, and thus easily offended.) Alas, this became known for many years as the 'Boccherini concerto', and virtually every cellist played it, not realising that it bore as much relation to Boccherini as Donald Duck to a white swan. No (further) comment. On the other hand, the only extant copy of the original Boccherini concerto is in Grützmacher's hand, so I suppose we have to be grateful for that; and we can carry over that same mixture of suspicion and gratitude towards his relationship with the Bach suites. True, he had the nerve – in a good way – to programme suites in their entirety; admirable, but how could they have sounded? He brought out a 'performer's edition' in which, among other outrages, he had the nerve – in a bad way – to transpose the sixth suite into G major. (Perhaps I'm just jealous. It must be easier, which would be nice, I admit; but it's wrong. A different sound-world altogether.) Aside from tempo and dynamic markings galore, as well as rhythms altered whenever he felt like it, he added and changed notes all over the place. In a letter to his publisher regarding his editions, he modestly explains:

My main purpose has been to reflect and to determine what these masters might have been thinking, and to set down all they, themselves, could have indicated ... I feel I have more right than all the others to do this work.

Moving fairly swiftly on from Herr Grützmacher, however, we come to the considerably less dubious figure of Pablo Casals.

Casals and the Suites

It was Casals who started to play the suites everywhere, in a blazingly successful mission to popularise them around the world. As an old man, he remembered how he'd first discovered them: at the age of thirteen, while studying at the music school in Barcelona, he was earning money by playing in a café with an ensemble; a highlight of each evening's fare would be a solo performance by the prodigy. In an attempt to vary his repertoire, young Pablo was constantly on the lookout for new pieces. One day his father arrived from Casals' home town, Vendrell, to visit his son. Pablo told his father of his need for fresh music:

> Together we set off on the search. For two reasons I shall never forget that afternoon. First, my father bought me my first full-size cello – how proud I was to have that wonderful instrument! Then we stopped at an old music shop near the harbour. I began browsing through a bundle of musical scores. Suddenly I came upon a sheaf of pages, crumpled and discoloured with age. They were unaccompanied suites by Johann Sebastian Bach – for the cello only! I looked at them with wonder: Six Suites for Violoncello Solo. What magic and mystery, I thought, were hidden in those words? . . . That scene has never grown dim.

The love affair that started that day (particularly impressive, since the edition he found was the dreaded Grützmacher version) was to infect music-lovers everywhere. It took Casals twelve years before he felt ready, as the twentieth century dawned, to perform a whole suite in public; but after that there was no stopping him. He swept aside the notion of them as études, convinced that they contained some of the most profoundly emotional music ever written (and certain that Mendelssohn and Schumann had made a grave error in adding piano parts to the violin works). For Casals, the suites 'are the very essence of Bach, and Bach is the essence of music'. His famous recordings of the six suites for EMI – the first time anyone had recorded any of the suites in its entirety – were made at a particularly traumatic period, between 1936 and 1939, when not only was the Second World War looming, but Casals' beloved homeland was being viciously torn asunder by the Spanish Civil War. Turning to Bach must have provided sorely needed comfort in his darkest hours – as Bach's music has done, and continues to do, for countless men and women through the centuries.

It took some time for Casals' efforts to bear fruit, but eventually almost every cellist, as well as many players of other instruments, came to consider the suites as central to their musical life. The new acolytes were by no means only musicians, however; through Casals' seventy-five years or so of impassioned missionary work, people all over the world and from all walks of life were converted – ranging from Queen Victoria (in 1899) to Golda Meir (to whom Casals played – memorably – the fifth Sarabande in 1973, when he was ninety-six).

The floodgates had been opened, and – at first gradually, then in a torrent – further recordings and editions started to appear. Furthermore, as the suites grew in popularity, so did the idea of writing for unaccompanied cello. After virtually nothing of musical interest from the nineteenth century, the twentieth was to see the composition of an increasing number of important works (Kodály, Hindemith, Reger, Bloch, Dallapiccola, Britten, Dutilleux, etc.), all showing, to a greater or lesser degree, the influence of the great Leipzig master. I hope that Bach, sitting in heaven, felt some satisfaction: after some two hundred years, his suites had finally taken their rightful place as one (six) of the pillars of Western civilisation.

THE MUSIC

PART 3

Dance Suites!

For all their profundity, the seemingly inexhaustible spectrum of emotions they encompass, the suites – with the exception of the Preludes – essentially consist of a collection of dance movements. Each of these movements is formed in accordance with the metric and rhythmic properties, the choreography, of the original dance. Therefore, it is worth exploring those properties, and the history behind them.

History of the Suite

It seems that the first use of the word 'suite' in a musical setting was a short sequence entitled 'suyttes de bransles', the 'bransle' or 'branle' being a French dance deriving its name, rather unpromisingly, from the word *branler*, meaning 'to shake, wave, sway, wag or wobble' – with rather ruder connotations, even today, in French slang. This pioneering work was published in 1557 by the French composer Estienne du Tertre, no less (though no more, either). The career of the branle endured for some time, the original branching off into stylised tributaries such as the Branle des Pois, the Branle des Hermites and the Branle du Chandelier, as well as the Branle Gay. However, as it began to take off in the seventeenth century, the musical suite as we know it increasingly omitted the poor branle. The published suites of the German composer Johann Jakob Froberger (1616–67) are credited with having established a standard series of dances: allemande, courante, sarabande, gigue. From there, other dances (some actually descended from that arch-progenitor Mr Branle) started to creep in between the sarabande and the gigue; these included the minuets, bourrées and gavottes that form the penultimate movements in the cello suites. In other baroque collections we find such diverse titles as passepieds, loures, airs or even polonaises, these extra movements initially referred to as 'galanteries'. Expanding the form still further, later suites were introduced by preludes, or overtures. All of Bach's cello suites open with preludes, his orchestral suites with overtures; of his twelve suites for keyboard, the six known as the 'English' suites also begin with preludes, while the so-called 'French' suites revert, like the first and second violin partitas, to the earlier suite form, all being launched by allemandes. (Incidentally, there is nothing 'English' about the English suites – they are only so-named because it was said that they were commissioned by an Englishman of rank, though we have no idea who that may have been. Meanwhile, just to inject a little bonus confusion, the only movement entitled 'Anglaise' within the twelve works is to be found in the third French suite.)

It is perhaps significant that the original meaning of the word 'suite' was 'a train of followers or attendants', accompanying a lord. If any of that original etymology survives into the musical form, then it is probably fair to say that the lord

of each of the cello suites, attended by his dancing courtiers,
is the Prelude . . .

The Movements

Preludes

As their name implies, preludes precede the other movements of a work, the word being derived from the Latin *prae*
(before) and *ludus* (play). This being the tale of the Bach
suites, however, it's not quite that simple: in German, the
word *präludieren* means to improvise; and it's true that by
the time the cello suites were composed, the prelude had
long been established as an independent, free-standing entity. The prelude's history stretches back to antiquity, in fact:
the Roman writer Quintilianus (*c.*35–100 AD) tells us that at
the musical competitions that were in vogue at the time, players of the lyre opened with preludes 'to win the favour of the
audience', before embarking upon an attempt to win the
prize. Well after Bach's era, it would become a hugely popular form in its own right, thanks to such masters as Chopin
and Rachmaninov – who also, in their spare time, humanised
the étude. (Bach's Chorale Preludes for organ had a related
function, being presented before the congregation sang the
chorale in question. His Preludes for organ were also played
in church before a service, or choral work, in order to induce
an appropriate frame of mind among the worshippers.)

The Preludes that launch the cello suites are thus weight-
ed with quite a few responsibilities: they are required to open
the door to the work as a whole, to establish the tonality, to

stand on their own as pieces of music, and even to incorporate some elements of improvisation. These particular Preludes are also intended to display the glories of the instrument – and by implication, the performer. (Mattheson refers to the execution of preludes in general as 'the highest peak of performance'.) All of these goals, needless to say, these Preludes attain – and far more.

It is posssibly no accident that the title page of Manuscript C announces the suites as 'Suiten und Preluden'. If this were a spoken tale, the Preludes would, I think, be presenting all the main characters in the story and giving us a clear idea of their characteristics (like an operatic overture in a way, although the Preludes are not charged with presenting the melodic themes of the upcoming work). Each Prelude reveals the overall tonal structure of the whole suite in question, by establishing not only the tonic, but also the hierarchy of related keys that will accompany that ruling tonality throughout all the movements. In this way, they play a key role, as it were, in introducing the essential emotional narrative of the entire work, the succeeding movements providing further aspects to the same journey. Each Prelude also explores a specific aspect of the cello's potential sonorities, from the gently lapping arpeggios of the first to the bell-like celebrations of the sixth. They also contain, in terms of rhythmic energy, dance elements; improvisatory though some of them may feel at times, I believe strongly that the tempo should be, for the most part, as clearly felt as in the other movements. All six Preludes represent a discrete voyage, moving from home (the tonic) through other lands (the satellite keys) before returning to base (bass). They are entirely satisfying musical structures in their own right, and yet at the same time, one can always feel that they are exactly as described on the tin: Preludes.

The Dances*

Many think of Bach as the archetypal German composer. Apart from a few works in Latin – notably the B minor Mass and the Magnificat – and a couple of cantatas in Italian, the texts of his entire vocal output are in German. Outwardly, in fact, he seems to have been thoroughly, solidly, beer-drinkingly Teutonic. Despite frequent short trips to local towns in order to test new organs, and some more extended forays – often, during his younger days, on foot – his travels never took him beyond his own area of central eastern Germany, known as Thuringia. (Perhaps the most notable of his journeys was a 280-mile walk in 1705 from Arnstadt to Lübeck in order to hear and meet the great Danish organist and composer Dietrich Buxtehude (c.1637–1707). It is possible that Buxtehude suggested Bach take over his highly prestigious job at Lübeck's famed Marienkirche – a tempting prospect for a twenty-year-old. If the offer was made, however, it would almost certainly have come with a strict condition: Bach must marry Buxtehude's eldest daughter. Like Handel and Mattheson before him, Bach refused the

---

* For some of the information in this chapter, I am indebted to a lovely book entitled *Dance and the Music of J. S. Bach* by Meredith Little and Natalie Jenne (Indiana University Press, 2001). They go into intriguing detail about each dance, illustrating the steps, phrase lengths, stresses, etc.

invitation; alas, one does suspect that the daughter's charms must have been somewhat limited ...)

Yet in addition to his solidly German, Lutheran credentials, Bach was also steeped in French (as well as Italian) culture. From the ages of fifteen to seventeen, he studied at a school in which the dancing master, Thomas de la Selle, was a pupil of the great Italian–French – but principally French – composer Jean-Baptiste Lully, a favourite at the court of Louis XIV, the 'Sun King'. It was this Lully who, famously and unfortunately, became rather carried away while directing an orchestral performance and drove into his foot the long staff with which he was beating the floor to keep time, resulting in gangrene (conducting is a dangerous art). He could have been saved, perhaps, had his leg been amputated; but Lully refused this, unable to tolerate a life without dancing – with the result that the poison spread throughout his body, and he died. One may conclude, therefore, that dance was important both to his life and to his music. The young Bach must have imbibed something of this attitude – if not to health, then to dance, first at school and then on subsequent visits to the court at a nearby town called Celle, a sort of 'miniature Versailles', where de la Selle was employed as a court musician (de la Selle de Celle, as it were). At Celle, Bach would have heard the orchestral music of Lully and the keyboard works of such French masters as François Couperin 'le Grand'. Indeed, we know from Forkel that Bach 'was acquainted with Couperin's works and esteemed them'. (My teacher used to say that unless we knew our Couperin, we couldn't hope to understand Bach – but maybe that was going a bit too far? Discuss.)

French dancing had spread from the court of Louis XIV throughout Europe; in fact, it was all the rage in Germany. Bach was personally acquainted with several Gallic dancing masters, who were much in demand at many of the courts he frequented. Not surprising, then, that his music would so often reflect that influence. Knowledge of the French language and culture implied sophistication; perhaps that is why the title pages of both Anna Magdalena's and Kellner's copies of the cello suites are predominantly written in French, as are the titles of the movements. (Well, most of them: Kellner occasionally strays into Italian, for some reason.) More important, however, is the fact that, whatever their actual provenance, the original dances on which the cello suites are based are largely French in character.

Allemandes

I believe that I speak for the majority of my colleagues when I say that the Allemandes are, from an interpretative point of view, the most challenging movements in the suites; that's why cellists will almost never choose to play one of them as an encore after a concerto performance. The Allemandes are hard to characterise convincingly – partly because they vary in tempo from one example to another to a greater degree than any of the other suite movements. Whereas one can confidently proclaim that, even though there is some disparity between their respective tempi, the Courantes in the suites are all pretty lively, the Sarabandes slow, etc., the Allemandes remain more of a puzzle. While the earlier ones are obviously to be played at something of a walking tempo, neither fast nor slow, the Allemande pulse seems to expand as the suites progress; by the sixth, it is clear that the beat is extremely spacious – in fact, Kellner marks it 'Adagio', sources C and D 'Molto adagio'. (At least the transformation is gradual, not sudden, as in other composers: within Corelli's set of twelve trio sonatas op. 2, for example, the Allemandes veer bewilderingly between utterly dissimilar tempi: 'Adagio' in sonata no. 2, 'Presto' in nos. 3 and 4, 'Allegro' in no. 5, 'Largo' in no. 6 – and so on.) Another nerdish dilemma: within our cello suites, in the Allemandes of suites nos. 1, 4 and 5, both Anna Magdalena and Kellner mark the time signature as 'alla breve'.* (Source C marks this only in the first Allemande, source D in none of them.) This would generally imply that the tempo should be faster than in a normal 4/4 – possibly twice as fast, even; but here I, for one, cannot imagine the fourth Allemande, for instance, being that much faster than the third. Perhaps it is merely indicating that there should be a clear two impulses to the bar, rather than four; but again, the fourth in particular does not seem to fit that bill, any more than the third. Yet another question with which to wrestle until I shuffle off these mortal curls.

Anyway, part of the problem with allemandes seems to be that by Bach's time they had become almost exclusively instrumental pieces, rather than dances. It's true that in Johann Gottfried Walther's *Musikalisches Lexikon* – which Bach must have known, since not only was it published in

* Alla breve – written like this: ₵ – tells us that a bar in 4/4 (indicated by the C) is to be thought of in two (illustrated by the vertical line through said C).

Leipzig in 1732, but Walther was in fact Bach's cousin – we read that allemandes 'must be composed and likewise danced in a grave and ceremonious manner'; but there are almost no choreographic guides to the allemande from the eighteenth century, as there are for the other dances that comprise the suites, implying that they were no longer part of the regular dance set that made up the programme for social and official evenings.

As its name implies, the allemande seems to have derived from Germany, even though the earliest written descriptions surface in France and Britain in the sixteenth century. In his vast, charmingly quirky and lavishly illustrated *Orchésographie* of 1588 – the inspiration, incidentally, for Peter Warlock's 1926 *Capriol* suite – the French dancing master Thoinot Arbeau (1520–95) tells us that the allemande is an ancient dance, describing it rather sniffily as 'une dance plaine de mediocre gravité'. He goes on to remark, gravely, that it is possible during an allemande for a gentleman to steal the lady partner of another, a practice of which he thoroughly (and quite rightly, of course) disapproves. The dance begins, according to Arbeau, with a step to the left, a step to the right, another step to the left, and a 'strike' with the right. French composers of the seventeenth century developed the allemande, generally slowing it down and transforming it into an expressive musical form. The keyboard works of Louis Couperin (1626?–61), for example, include allemandes 'de la paix', 'la Precieuse', 'grave' and 'l'Amiable'; his nephew François continued this noble family tradition by producing allemandes with such names as 'l'Auguste', 'la Laborieuse' (doesn't sound very promising) and, more alluringly, 'l'Exquise'. By Bach's time, Mattheson – who, in contrast to Arbeau, considered the allemande 'an upright German invention' – was demanding from the music 'serious and well-composed harmoniousness . . . delighting in order and calm'. The Allemandes of the cello suites certainly satisfy those last criteria, but in such varied fashion. The one element that appears to unite all six is the basic metric structure: both halves beginning with an upbeat of one or three notes, and thenceforth, in general, a strong first beat (maybe the 'strike' has shifted?), weak second beat, and third and fourth beats leading back to the next bar. As with almost all the other dance movements of the suites, there are two sections; except for those of the fourth and sixth suites, the two parts of the Allemandes are of equal length. Allemandes tend to be, along with the Sarabandes, the most 'grown-up', well-tended dance movements of the cello suites.

I think that's all I have to say about allemandes for the moment, so let's now turn, perhaps with some relief, to their less complex relation (friend? neighbour?), the courante.

Courantes

The title of this dance implies 'running'; and indeed all the Courantes of the cello suites are vigorous in nature. But – needless to say – it's not quite as straightforward as that. There are in fact two distinct types of courante: the French and the Italian (the latter sometimes known as *corrente*, but not spelled as such in any of the cello suite sources). True, both types contain fast-running notes, but they are diverse

both in metre and in the speed of the beat. The French courante is generally in 3/2, and the tempo – if counted in those
three beats – is supposed to be the slowest of all baroque
dances, even though, due to the rapid notes, it tends to feel
like a fast movement. It must have been the French type that
Bach's cousin Walther had in mind when he described the
rhythm of the courante as 'the most serious one can find'.
Louis XIV is said to have practised this dance daily for
twenty-two years; according to the composer Jean-Philippe
Rameau (1683–1764) – he of whom it was said that from his
deathbed he rebuked the priest for bad intonation while
chanting the last rites – the king danced it better than any of
his courtiers. (Not necessarily an unbiased opinion?)
François Couperin again gives us a clue to the varying nature
of the form, differentiating in one of his Concerts Royaux of
1722 between a French courante, to be played 'noblement',
and an Italian one, 'gayement'. The steps of a danced French
courante are slow and dignified – including a gliding motion
– whereas the choreography for the Italian dance involves
some rather less exalted hopping and skipping.

Of the Courantes in the cello suites, only the fifth, in C
minor, conforms to the French type; it is in 3/2 metre, with a
spacious beat. The others, all in 3/4 and with a greater number of bars, are Italian in nature (with the partial exception of
the second, the D minor, which, with its more serious character and slightly slower pulse, leans somewhat towards the
French manner). Anyway, the two alternative forms do have
elements in common: the shared liveliness of spirit, expressed
in the short, running notes within each beat, and the frequent

quirkiness of the rhythmic stresses. Maybe the French and Italians have more in common than initially meets the eye – or ear, at least.

Sarabandes

Like majestically beating hearts at the centre of each suite, the Sarabandes are oases of poignant calm, the points at which the listener is most likely to be reduced to tears. Nobility and poise radiate from every musical pore of all six. The sarabande was not always so virtuous, however: thought to have originated in Central America in the first half of the sixteenth century, the early sarabande was a vivacious, even lascivious, affair, often danced with castanets and frowned upon by respectable citizens; it bore little resemblance to its descendants, except for being in triple time (the metre was always in three). Even in those days of more limited travel, this reprehensible cavort soon managed to cross the seas – as dangerously infectious substances will. Much to the dismay of some, the sarabande became highly popular in Europe. In the early 1600s, the influential Spanish priest Juan de Mariana bewailed the fact that it could 'excite bad emotions even in thoroughly decent people'; it was officially banned in Spain from 1583. Nevertheless, the dance found its way to France, and to Germany; in his 1612 collection of dances entitled *Terpsichore*, the German composer Michael Praetorius (1571–1621), interestingly (I think), includes a couple of 'Courante Sarabandes' – curious when by Bach's time the two dances had grown so far apart, their only similarity being the three beats to a bar. Over the generations the sarabande, thankfully, mutated into a slow and dignified affair, putting its stormy adolescent years behind it (rather like Bach himself?), and maturing towards the sublime examples found within the suites. The choreography could by this time include almost imperceptible glides and magical moments of immobility.

François Couperin, always a good source for descriptive titles, gives his keyboard sarabandes such intriguing designations as 'la Majestueüse', 'la Lugubre', 'la Dangereuse', even 'la Prude'. These sarabandes from the latter years of the baroque period – those of Couperin, Bach and many others – invariably open with a bar of strong first and second beats; thereafter, the metric accents may vary, with frequent use of the hemiola, a triple-time cadential device much used in baroque (and other) music in which the beats give the impression of changing from the basic *one*-two-three in one bar to *one*-two-*three*-one-*two*-three over two bars. This expands the rhythmic flow, giving the music – and us – the space to pause and reflect. It's not surprising that when a cellist plays a Bach movement as an encore, it is most likely to be one of the Sarabandes. Bach clearly loved the genre: no surprise that he wrote more of them than of any other type of dance.

Minuets (suites 1 and 2)

The minuet also comprises three beats to the bar, and begins on the downbeat; but apart from that it has little in common with the sarabande. Its nature is livelier, and the second beats tend to be light, rather than stressed. Also, further differentiating the two dances, there is a definite feeling here of one large beat to each bar. The minuet was the only baroque dance to survive in full musical health into the classical era, forming the third part of countless four-movement symphonic, sonata and chamber structures of that period, only gradually being replaced by the scherzo (Italian for 'joke'). In those later examples, the minuets are almost always accompanied by a contrasting 'trio' section; these movements-within-movements acquired that title because in orchestral works earlier composers such as Lully – who wrote no fewer than ninety-two minuets, the addict – would pare down the orchestration to three instruments. (This can be a bit puzzling, in fact, since these sections continued to be called trios even when that reduced instrumentation was abandoned. I once arranged three trio sections from Haydn symphonies for four cellos – but felt that it would have been a tad confusing to entitle them 'three trios for quartet'.) Bach, however, generally wrote, as in the cello suites, pairs of two contrasting minuets – simpler, for once.

The French minuets of the seventeenth and eighteenth centuries, as danced at court, must have been elegant affairs. The dancers would bow to the king (of course) and to each other, then retire to diagonally opposite corners of the dance floor, before performing several figures, each requiring six dance-steps, outlining the letter Z. At one point, they would meet in the centre of the room, grasp the others' right hands, circle around each other and return to opposite corners. There is some argument as to the general nature of the minuet: in his 1703 *Dictionnaire de musique* – one of the first of its kind – the ábbé Sébastien de Brossard (1655–1730) tells us that the minuet is 'always very gay and very fast'; some sixty years later, however, Jean-Jacques Rousseau (1712–78), no less, argues that

This is not quite right. The character of the Minuet is a noble and elegant simplicity; the movement is moderate rather than quick. It may be said that the least gay of all the kinds of dances used at our balls is the minuet.

A conundrum, then; but it does seem as if a played minuet could be taken at a slower tempo than the danced version. Bach's examples certainly seem rather to follow Rousseau's assessment, the two pairs in the cello suites requiring (I feel, anyway – some might disagree strongly) the same moderate tempo, but contrasted in both mood and mode: the second Minuet of the first suite is in G minor, rather than the overall G major; the second Minuet of the D minor suite (no. 2) is in D major. Along with the second Bourrée of the third suite (C minor instead of C major), these second Minuets are the only movements in the entire cycle not to be in the home key of the suite as a whole.

Incidentally, all of the varying fifth movements – Minuets, Bourrées, Gavottes – are written in 'da capo' form, a common practice for those double movements: one plays the first of the pair, with repeats, then the second, also with repeats, and then one goes back and plays the first again. And here again is a bone over which musicologists tussle: should one repeat the repeats of the first when one plays it for the second time? Players these days usually omit them; but there are examples in other works of the period in which the composer has instructed the performer to repeat the first minuet *senza repetizione* – or words to that effect – implying that without that directive, the players of the time would indeed have included the repeats in the da capo. This possibility is bolstered by the fact that the danced minuet was extremely long; from a musical point of view, however, it is questionable, tending to try the patience of the listener (the modern listener, at any rate). So again, a matter for much discussion – not the most exciting of arguments, perhaps; but it can keep a nerd like me happy – and frequently indignant – for hours on end. More fun than worrying about one's overdraft, anyway . . .

Bourrées (suites 3 and 4)

The bourrée (known at one time in England as a 'borry' or, rather unfortunately, 'bore') is a thoroughly friendly dance. Mattheson writes that 'its essential characteristic is contentment, pleasantness, unconcern' – a good person to have at a party, in fact (or dance to include within a suite, anyway). In his *Terpsichore*, Michael Praetorius includes it under the category of branle, from which it is descended. Originating in the Auvergne – still danced there today – and introduced to the French court as early as 1565, it maintained its popularity in the court of Louis XIV. It also gave its name to a graceful ballet step, *pas de bourrée*, which involves a gentle movement while poised on tiptoe. I'm not sure that one can feel any trace of that in Bach's bourrées – at least not in those of the cello suites; but they do offer an intriguing mixture of characters, grouped as they are in – again – vividly contrasted pairs.

The bourrée starts with a crotchet-length upbeat, consisting of one, two or four notes. It is generally marked in 4/4, but in effect has two beats; many bourrées are marked alla breve. In the cello suites, we are presented with our usual confusing array of different alternatives on this issue: Anna Magdalena marks all four Bourrées alla breve, except for the last, the second of the fourth suite; Kellner marks all four alla breve; source C one of each pair – the second of suite 3, the first of suite 4; and source D none of them. So – as always – we have to take our pick. (Though maybe in the end it makes little or no difference.)

A small footnote: Bach's most famous bourrée is probably the one from his E minor suite for lute. This innocent little tune is said to have inspired not only Schumann, but also Jethro Tull, Led Zeppelin and Paul McCartney (for 'Blackbird'). Pity that it was out of copyright by then; Bach could have afforded all the alcoholic beverages his heart desired.

Gavottes (suites 5 and 6)

The gavotte is a close descendant of the branle; in fact, Monsieur Arbeau describes it as being comprised of a mixture of branles. He also, in his instructions, advises that, a couple having danced the gavotte, the gentleman 'kisses all the other ladies, and his lady all the young men'. Sounds extremely dubious, and somewhat unhygienic; happily, that particular custom was later replaced by one of presenting flowers. The gavotte was especially popular in Bach's time, its regularity and order perhaps representing a bucolic ideal for which the metropolitan sophisticates told themselves that they yearned.

Gavottes contain either two or four beats per bar, like the bourrée; some earlier examples begin on the downbeat of the bar, but by Bach's time the gavotte had acquired a half-bar upbeat. This, unlike the crotchet-length upbeat to the bourrées, counts as a beat in its own right, rather than a mere precursor. The four examples of gavottes in the cello suites are again highly contrasted, having little in common other than this basic rhythmic structure. However, there is one striking feature that does permeate all of them. When the gavotte was danced, music and movement tended to be quite independent, only coinciding as the dancers landed heavily on the first beat of the fourth bar; one can quite clearly feel this sense of arrival at that point in most phrases of these gavottes.

Bach experimented with the form, one movement of his E major partita for violin being a 'Gavotte en rondeau', the basic dance being interspersed with varying episodes. The cello Gavottes, occurring only in the last two suites, are also quite experimental, Bach by this point in the cycle having transcended (though not abandoned) the comparatively simple versions of the dances with which he'd begun. Again, the sources can't agree on a time signature: Anna Magdalena and Kellner mark all four movements as alla breve; source C marks just the first Gavotte of the sixth suite as alla breve, while writing a 2 (i.e. 2/2) for the second; and source D has no alla breve, just the same 2 for the second Gavotte of the sixth. Would that 2 mean the same as alla breve? I'd have thought so; but then why has source C seemingly differentiated between the two? I don't know. Then again, does it matter? And again – I just don't know . . .*

Gigues

The gigue (or giga, or jig) is generally the least courtly, but often the most energetic, of all the dances in the suites, invariably placed at the end of the work. By Bach's time, the gigue was probably (at least in polite circles) thought of as an instrumental form: the French writer Sébastien de Brossard describes it as an 'air ordinarily for instruments . . . full of pointed and syncopated notes which render the piece gay and, so to speak, skipping [*sautillant*]'.

The gigue seems to have been derived from wild British country jigs; since it was often accompanied by fiddles, it is also said to have given the violin its German name, 'Geige'. It also goes under different titles: the 'lourié', for instance, a slower dance of which there are two examples in Bach, also qualifies as a gigue. Another category is the 'canary' – so-called either because it derives from the Canary Islands, or (in Arbeau's preferred version) from a masque in which two dancers played the king and queen of Mauritania, or else unnamed shapely savages, with multicoloured (hence canary-like) plumage. This dance was popular enough in England for Shakespeare to allude to it in *All's Well That Ends Well*, in which a character tells the king of a medicine:

* John Butt, who *does* know – seemingly – virtually everything about Bach, suggests that the '2' marking 'can perhaps be summed up as "more French" – or perhaps "more up-to-date"' (same thing, of course).

That's able to breathe life into a stone
Quicken a rock, and make you dance canary,
With sprightly fire and motion.

The jig itself also makes a few appearances in Shakespeare –
as in *Much Ado About Nothing*, in which Beatrice sarcastically
refers to a lover's initial wooing as 'hot and hasty like a Scotch
jig'. (Even the 'coranto' gets a mention in *Twelfth Night*.)

Beginning with a short upbeat, and set in so-called 'compound time' – any time signature in which the beats are usually divided into three rather than two – later gigues are again
split into French and Italian types, with many subdivisions.
The French variety contains frequent dotted rhythms – so
within the cello suites, only the Gigue of the fifth qualifies as
such. The Gigues of the minor-key suites, 2 and 5, are in 3/8
time, resulting in a greater terseness, and one impulse per
bar; the others are all in 6/8, giving rise therefore to two
impulses.

By Bach's time, although generally high-spirited
(depending, as in the suites, on the overall character of the
work), the gigue had become far more sophisticated than its
antecedents, those for keyboard frequently containing fugal
passages. Nevertheless, and despite any number of varying
moods, it never loses its buoyant vigour, providing a fitting
conclusion – in all of Bach's many examples, at least – to a
suite.

PART 4

Questions and Rules (the didactic section)

The Bach suites seem to awaken the curiosity of listeners to an extraordinary degree. It follows, therefore, that performers will be asked a number of questions about them on a regular basis. Here are some of the ones I have encountered frequently, along with some of the typical answers I tend to give:

Answers to Fourteen Frequently Asked Questions

1. 'What makes the Bach suites so special?'

This is a tricky one. We can certainly point to Bach's amazing feat in exploiting the possibilities of the cello to the full, with, it seems, no examples before him to provide guidance. Nowhere is the cello expected to produce a sound contrary to its nature, and yet the sonorities are as full as the music requires; at no point does one miss the presence of another instrument, Bach transforming the limitations of his materials into a limitless strength. In addition, there is another, less obvious element at work here. I once asked the late Frans Brüggen how I should reply when asked this question; he thought for a moment, and then said (I hope I'm quoting him correctly – I think I am): 'Tell them that it's because of the invisible bassline.' It's true: the music is guided, propelled by this extraordinary foundation, sometimes sounded, sometimes implied – but hardly less present for that – and always so full of life and interest. But I suppose that the ultimate answer has to be that through these outwardly simple dance suites Bach takes us on an emotional/spiritual journey like no other, leading us from pastoral joy through to profound tragedy, before concluding in jubilation and triumph. Each listener will experience this journey differently, of course; but for all those to whom the music speaks, it will be life-changing in some way.

2. *'Do you try to play in a baroque style, or modern?'*

Hmm . . . tricky again. (This is why I tend to avoid too much conversation after I've played a suite.) The first thing to say is that I don't 'try' to play in any specific style; my chief aim is to respond to the music naturally. After all, Bach would surely have expected just that; as the great violinist/conductor Sándor Végh used to say: 'Mozart didn't know he was writing in the style of Mozart!' That's slightly fudging the issue, though, I have to admit; there are certainly stylistic questions to be addressed here. But first, what *is* 'baroque style'? Can we really believe that everybody played in the same way, in different countries, even in different towns – not to mention different players? (What a silly expression that is, 'not to mention'; it invariably means that you're just about to mention the subject in question.) True, there are many contemporary treatises, of which one must be aware; but again – how representative are they, and of whom? If a writer today were to compose a manual advising young musicians how to play the music of our time, it's quite likely, for instance, that they would advise using vibrato sparingly; and yet most of today's players use it pretty much continuously. So do we wish to recreate how instrumentalists of the day played (if we could); or to follow the tracts of the period – which usually contradict each other anyway? I think that the answer is to educate ourselves as widely as possible, reading all the materials we can find, and then to follow our – now refined – instincts. I have a strong feeling (impossible to prove, of course) that if one had asked Bach to sing a phrase from his music, it would have come out sounding pretty much as that phrase would sound today, if produced naturally.

3. 'Do you ever play the baroque cello?'

The answer to this is basically 'no', though I have occasionally experimented with one. I do listen frequently to baroque instruments, however, and learn a lot from doing so; indeed, there are many works from the period that I really prefer to hear on those instruments. As for the Bach suites: I believe that there are both gains and losses from playing it on a 'modern' cello – or rather, on a cello with a modern set-up. (Many players of today, myself included, play on instruments made during Bach's lifetime, albeit set up in the new manner.) One gains, I think, a warmth and richness that is quite appropriate for the spirit of Bach's art; on the other hand, one can all too easily be tempted by these enhanced potential sonorities into a sound-world inappropriate to the character of the music. Furthermore, playing on the baroque cello, and particularly with a baroque bow, can both suggest and facilitate appropriate articulations and phrasings. The question of pitch is also important: Bach's orchestral instruments would have been tuned far lower than today's. (With the caveat here that there seems to have been at that time a bewildering array of tunings in different towns; some of the organs Bach played were actually tuned considerably higher than today's instruments. The pitches used in Köthen and Leipzig were much lower than our modern ones, however.) Today's players who tune their violins and cellos down to 'baroque' pitches for performances of the solo works say that their instruments feel freer, which I can well believe; on the other hand, the sound lacks the same brilliance – though perhaps that doesn't matter much? A decision for each player – and each listener, when it comes to choice of performances or recordings – to make for themselves.

The analogy I tend to use is of an actor who tries to recreate Shakespearean pronunciation in performances of the Bard's plays: some features certainly fall into place (rhymes, etc.), while other aspects become more difficult for a modern audience to grasp. Finally, I don't think it makes *that* much difference: Lear is still betrayed by his elder daughters, Hamlet still has to wrestle with his indecision, etc. The core of the meaning is not changed; and the same goes for the harmonic journey, the emotional message of the suites, on whichever instrument they may be played. The sonorities are a by-product of the essence, not – as in some music – the essence itself.

It's also worth pointing out that modern string instruments are by no means as different from their baroque ancestors as modern pianos are from the keyboard instruments available to Bach – even the early fortepianos with which he became familiar towards the end of his life. Not that I disapprove in any way of performances of Bach on the modern piano – far from it; but its sonorities are absolutely unlike any sound Bach would have heard. By contrast, the violins, cellos, etc. that we mostly hear today are the same shape, even occupy the same basic sound-world, as their older counterparts. True, there are major differences: the set-up – neck-length, bass-bar, etc. – of today's string instruments has changed; and modern cellists, unlike those of Bach's time, use spikes, or endpins, which alter one's physical approach to playing. But a cello is still a cello – whereas a piano is definitely *not* a harpsichord.

The bow and strings are another matter. Today's bow-hold, as well as the bow itself, is different; and so are the strings, which in Bach's time were made of sheep-gut, whereas most of today's players use steel strings. Here I stand with the baroque players (even though my usually aluminium-covered gut strings are, I'm sure, quite unlike the raw gut ones of Bach's day). There's a basic difference between all types of gut strings and their steel rivals, the former more mellow and earthy in sound, the latter, it's true, more brilliant and penetrating; but surely one doesn't need to be penetrating in Bach? This is music for self-communion more than for noisy projection. For me personally, it is something of a mini-religion: In Gut We Trust. (Or, as the comedian Barry Humphries once put it: 'It takes guts to be a cellist.')

4. *'Do the suites sound better in a concert hall or a church?'*

Well, although there is no record of the suites having been performed at Köthen, it is pretty certain that if they were, it would have been at court, not in a chapel. In Leipzig, if they were played at all, it was probably in a coffee-house or in Bach's own home. So perhaps they are intended more for the private concert hall – or chamber – than for the church. It does seem likely, however, that most spacious rooms in those days would have been more reverberant than today's, which would have been useful for the softer sonorities of the instruments of the time. (I suspect that people also had better ears then, with less noise surrounding them all day long.) The suites certainly benefit from a warm acoustic, allowing the cello to ring out freely; the sound in some modern concert halls can lack bloom. So I'd say that either hall or church is fine, providing that there is enough resonance – but not so much of an echo that details become blurred.

5. *'Were the suites performed with dancers during Bach's lifetime?'*

Certainly not that we know of; and I'd be very surprised if they were used in that way. As mentioned earlier, we have no record of any performance of them at all until the nineteenth century; but if they were played, I'm pretty sure it would have been in a concert (private or public) setting, not as an accompaniment. Some cellists today have performed them with dancers; it can be interesting – and at least it means that the cellist has to play in time! But I myself – as listener or player – don't want to be distracted from the music; one should be able to imagine the dance, if one wishes to do so. The music, as I see it, is inspired by the spirit, the metric rules, of the original dances; but it doesn't require their presence.

6. 'Why is it so scary to play the Bach suites?'

It *is* scary to perform the suites. For me personally (but not just for me, by any means), the memory aspect is terrifying: I'm always convinced that I'm going to forget the next note. But there is also the sheer unadulterated exposure of sitting by oneself onstage, with nothing to hide one's failings. Of course, pianists do that all the time, when they give solo recitals, but at least they don't have to face the audience! Also, it is easier for them to add harmonies as they flail around in panic when they lose their way. More than that, though, it's the responsibility. The suites are so perfect, and yet somehow so vulnerable, that one is desperate not to let them down. I remember thinking, on the two occasions on which I performed the cycle at my 'musical home', the Wigmore Hall in London: 'I am playing perfect music, on a perfect Stradivarius cello, with a perfect Tourte bow, in a perfect space. The only element of failure that can intrude and ruin it all is – me.' Gulp. (Of course, it is also an ecstatic, joyous experience like no other – when it goes well . . .)

7. 'Why do you feel you have to play them from memory?'

Well, maybe it's silly, but I do find a music stand somehow impedes contact with the audience in these pieces – though not in all music, by any means. But more important is that the voyage of each suite really begins from the first note, and ends with the last; there is no time to turn pages. (It's funny to see Anna Magdalena's and Kellner's instructions – 'Voltecito' or 'Volti subito' ['turn quickly'] – in the middle of movements; that would completely ruin the performance.) So other than using iPads and the like – the mere thought of which sends me into a blind panic – the only option would be having someone there to turn the pages. I did play the fourth suite once with a page-turner; but he turned consistently one movement ahead of the one I was actually playing – so I had to play it from memory after all. I found, in fact, that I could do it – so I thanked him; he'd done me a favour.

8. 'Since there are almost no tempo or dynamic indications in any of the manuscripts, how do you know which tempi to take and which dynamics to insert?'

It's pretty common in baroque music to have very few, if any, such directions. The solution is simply to look inside the music; if one looks hard enough, it should tell you what to do. The dynamics are controlled largely by the bassline, whether sounded or not; it governs the direction of the phrases, and hence the dynamics. Some of the suites – the first and second, for instance – obviously start softly; others, such as the third and sixth, loudly. (The latter is actually marked – well, implied – in three of the four sources by a *piano* in the second bar, meaning that the first must be *forte*.) From those beginnings, the rest should just fall into place; it is all so clear and logical. The same with tempo: it should be determined by the character of the dance, obviously, but also by the rate of harmonic change, which will have its own innate flow; and I find that once one has played one movement at a certain tempo, the rest will follow naturally. That's why it is quite hard to play a dance movement from any of the suites out of context; it is so dependent on what has preceded it. There may well be a mathematical relationship between the tempi of the movements, but I've never tried to work it out; it should, I feel, be subconscious and spontaneous, not planned.

9. 'Has your playing of the suites changed over the years – and if so, how?'

Yes, I'm sure that it has – but I couldn't describe the changes. It's like ageing: if one looks in the mirror every day, one doesn't perceive any difference; but then one sees a photo of oneself taken a few years ago, and one realises with a jolt that one is no longer the same ... groan ...

10. 'What do you think about when you play the suites?'

Well, partly what the next note will be (see above), and partly about images from the narrative that I believe may possibly have inspired the suites (see below). Most important, though, is to *listen* while one plays, to follow the musical journey, to hear the stories that Bach is telling us. And that's why one must be on top of the instrumental difficulties – so that one has the absolute freedom to listen as one plays. That, for me, constitutes a proper technique.

11. 'Do you have a favourite among the suites?'

No; the whole set is indispensable. It's true that the suites expand and become more elaborate, and more challenging, as they progress, the sixth being almost twice as long as the first; but to do without the first, or any of them, or to choose – impossible. Like dispensing with one of six children.

12. 'Do we have any evidence of how Bach would have wanted the suites played, apart from the manuscript copies?'

Not really, unless you count the playing manuals of the time. But Forkel, relying on reports given by those who heard Bach perform, gives a succinct description of Bach's own playing, which I think gives us quite a clear image, and is worth bearing in mind:

When he played his own music Bach usually adopted a brisk pace. He contrived to introduce so much variety that every piece became a sort of conversation between its parts. If he wished to express deep emotion he did not strike the notes with great force, as many do, but expressed his feeling in simple melodic and harmonic figures, relying rather on the internal resources of his art than external dynamics. Therein he was right. True emotion is not suggested by hitting the keyboard.

13. 'Is there humour in the suites?'

Absolutely! They're full of humour, especially suites 3 and 4. The humour ranges from cheerfulness to actual laugh-out-loud wit. This music has everything.

14. 'Does the word "suite" have anything to do with "sweet"?'

No.

Rules for the Player

It is not for me, or anyone else, to dictate how Bach's music should be interpreted; each player should have his or her individual approach. Frequently, however, I feel that unnecessary complications are brought into the performance of his music. I therefore offer the following highly debatable (and possibly rather annoying) nuggets of advice – principally focusing on the cello suites, but hopefully more or less applicable for any musician who plays Bach.

Rule 1: There are NO rules for playing this music – music this free and original transcends any restriction whatsoever.

Rule 2: Don't demonstrate your ideas! Many performances are ruined by them. Have ideas, by all means, but don't give us a lecture-recital. We want to hear the music as if it is being composed as you play, as if it's travelling through you unhindered by prefabricated theories.

Rule 3: Dance! Aside from the Preludes – but not excluding them either, in terms of rhythmic energy – these are *dance* suites (or, for the violin or keyboard, partitas or sonatas or whatever: there's always a sense of dance, even in the fugues). It is often said, with some justification, that the chief mode of expression on the harpsichord – one of Bach's principal instruments, of course – is through rubato; but even there, that does not mean that performances should have no tempo. *Rubato in tempo* is an essential component of music-making, so that it sounds spontaneous, but still has a clear, steady beat; as Casals used to put it: 'Freedom – with order!' The rhythms in a performance of the suites should induce in the audience members a desire to get up and dance – not make them feel seasick. It's good to remember a contemporary description of Bach conducting: he was 'full of rhythm in every part of his body'.

Rule 4: By all means read all you can about Bach, about his music, the playing styles and players of the era – you should, in fact; but don't let your knowledge ruin your performance. Never go against your instincts. True, instincts need educating; one couldn't really leave it to one's instincts to guess, for instance, that when Bach writes certain dotted rhythms, he would assume that the player would lengthen the long note, shorten the little one(s) – the convention known as 'double-dotting'. Hopefully, though, your instincts, on learning that, will exclaim: 'Aha – that makes sense.' (Because it does: think, for instance, of the opening section of the fifth suite; it would sound far too heavy without the double-dots that are a feature of its 'French overture' style – at least, I think it would.) Always listen to what the music is telling you, not to what you've read in a book or heard others do; ideally, you should play the music as you would sing it in the shower. It can be very useful to sing a phrase and then play it for comparison. (Another word of advice, though: don't take your cello into the shower to test this.)

Rule 5: If you haven't already done so, but have the possibility to play on an instrument from Bach's time, set up in a way he would have recognised, seize the opportunity. This can give you a feeling for a different approach, both musically and physically (not that the two can really be separated).

Rule 6: Ornamentation – if the spirit takes you, feel free to add some ornaments here or there, by all means; but again, don't feel that you *have* to add them, because 'it was done' then. Bach was not like many other composers of the period, who left much of the material to the player's fancy; he was aiming for (and of course achieved) perfection in his scores. In fact, he was critical of the French keyboard composers for being 'too affected in their frequent use of graces, which goes so far that scarcely a note is free of embellishments'. So, if you feel that a trill or appoggiatura here or there will increase the expression of a certain gesture, there's no need to hold back (and it is well worth looking at the ornaments written into sources C and D); but don't distort the line or rhythm with your additions. Remember that much of the ornamentation is marked into the music already. In fact, when the unfortunate Mr Scheibe made his lamentable attack on Bach in 1737, one of his complaints was that 'every note, every little grace, and everything that one thinks of as belonging to the method of playing, he expresses completely in notes'. That rather says it all; and even C. P. E. Bach, whose music is generally quite open to embellishment, muses that

> Many variants of melodies introduced by executants in the belief that they honour a piece, actually occurred to the composer, who, however, selected and wrote down the original because he considered it the best of its kind . . . A friend of mine takes every last pain to play pieces as written, purely and in accord with the rules of good performance. Can applause be rightfully denied him?

Rule 7: Meanwhile, talking of ornamentation: vibrato. A tricky one, this. I think we can be pretty sure that the players of Bach's time did not employ as much or as constant a vibrato as most modern players use today – even if the Italian violinist and composer Francesco Geminiani (1687–1762) tells us, around the time of Bach's death, that vibrato makes 'the sound more agreeable and should therefore be made use of as often as possible'. It was evidently thought of as a form of ornament itself, existing to enhance the expressive possibilities of the music, not as an automatic component of a player's sound. So again, I'd advise: if you feel that a note needs vibrato, then vibrate; but make sure that the vibrato truly comes from your heart, not just your finger. (Beware, however: if you're like me, your vibrato tends to become less controlled when you're nervous.) And be careful not to vibrate on 'weak' notes. It is generally only the stronger notes that benefit from the emphasis of vibrato in this music; emphasising the wrong ones distorts the phrasing. Then – trills: there are those who say that every (or almost every) baroque trill should start on the upper note; and those who hotly dispute that, affirming that if one has just played the upper note, or is about to play it, then the trill should start on the main note. I'd say that it depends on the sentiment you wish to express through the trill, as well as the clarity of line you wish to maintain. Sometimes you will want to feel the dissonance, the clash of the upper note before it resolves onto the main one, sometimes not. That, and also the speed of the trill, is the sort of thing you can certainly vary on repeats, along with the dynamics, phrasing, etc. – again, whatever the music suggests to you as you listen.

Rule 8: Let your bow dance too – and breathe! For me, there's always a sense of lightening of the bow at the bar line (unless it's slurred over); by this I do not mean a noticeable silence or diminuendo – just enough of an imperceptible breath to allow the first beat to have something of a fresh impulse. As I've often said to students: 'I'm sure you're going out and having fun at parties every night – let your bows have fun too.' And don't suffocate the poor things by pinning them to the string mercilessly – I'm surprised that some of them don't go blue in the stick.

Rule 9: Always be conscious of the beat of the bar on which you're playing. This sounds obvious, but one can easily forget – particularly in a slower movement, such as the Allemande of the sixth suite. While the metric stresses of the individual dances vary considerably, the first beat of the bar is never unimportant. It's not always heavy, of course, but it's generally a pivotal point of some kind, whether clearly stressed or not. A question about phrasing can often be clarified by following the metric shape of the dance. And avoid too many equal beats. They can kill the music; nothing makes a performance sound more static (and therefore boring) than a series of identical stresses.

Rule 10: Think about the bassline! Sometimes Bach writes it in, sometimes it's an invisible, unplayed, but strangely audible foundation underpinning and regulating the melodic voice above. If you have access to a keyboard instrument, and can play it to an even elementary level, play the suites through, adding the bassline where necessary. (Particularly useful in a movement such as the Prelude to the second suite, with so very few chords.) This will solve a lot of problems – and I think you'll find it easier than it may sound on paper, because it's so obvious when a bass note is wrong.

Rule 11: Further to that: you really *have* to work out a (very basic, at least) harmonic analysis of each movement you play. The story of the music lies in that journey through tonalities – composers think in harmonies. I do feel it's essential for the musician to look closely into how a work has been composed, because that is the only way to enter the head – and thus the heart and soul – of a composer. It's really not complicated. I can say that from personal experience: although I did take some harmony lessons, I absorbed more from studying the scores of works I was playing, because these make everything clear. Many composers would say the same, that they learned their craft from getting to know music of the past – including Bach, who was obviously inspired and educated by copying out the music of other composers. Any knowledge you acquire – again, it's a question of educating your instincts – will help to reveal the shape, the flow and ultimately the meaning of the music. Without understanding the harmonic direction, you're travelling in a foreign land without a guidebook – and with only a superficial grasp of the language. Remember that though this music may be democratic, everything in its allotted place, it is not egalitarian. There are heavy notes, light notes, notes of arrival – with notes of direction either moving towards or falling away from them – melody notes, accompanying notes, etc. As in speech, in fact – only machines talk in monotone syllables. Understanding the function of each note is crucial – and not hard.

Rule 12: Be careful how you play your chords: there are a lot of them, and they must neither scrunch nor distort the rhythms. Here, if playing with a modern set-up, it is useful to have in mind baroque instruments and bows, imagining the gentler approach one can take with the flatter bridges and lighter bows with their curved sticks. (I have to say that violinists often offend worse than cellists in this regard – understandably perhaps, since Bach demands much more from them chord-wise, especially when he's writing multi-voiced fugues. I've heard performances in which the grinding, scratch-laden chords made me long for the safety of a nuclear shelter – and I'm sure that shouldn't be strictly necessary.)

Rule 13: When one has worked out the bowings for any of these works, always bearing in mind the various patterns suggested by the sources, one may find that they're quite awkward to execute, and may leave one in the wrong part of the bow. Always try to make the music sound naturally flowing, not garbled – even if it involves some 'cheating', often by separating two notes within the same bow (as in, for example, playing two separated down-bows for the first two notes of a group of four semiquavers phrased in units of one and three). Whatever Bach meant by his articulations, I'm quite sure he didn't mean them to sound clumsy.

Rule 14: Having said all that: ENJOY the music – and be yourself! Don't be scared of Bach – he's not scared of you. Don't put him on a pedestal; the music may be divinely inspired, but it's also deeply human – and lots of fun. Of course, there are dark aspects, particularly in the two minor-mode suites (and at various points in the partitas/ sonatas), but even they shouldn't be depressing in any way. And there is so much joy and humour – albeit elevated humour. It's worth remembering – again – Forkel's words: 'Notwithstanding the main tendency of his genius for the great and sublime, he sometimes composed and performed something light-hearted and even jocose.' (He is quick to point out, however, that Bach's 'cheerfulness and joking were those of a sage'.)

A little musical diversion: Bach's name written in four different clefs, in the shape of a cross. In the treble clef, if one adds a flat to the key signature, as on the left, that middle note is B flat (i.e. B in German); in the tenor clef (on top) it is A; in the alto clef (to the right and upside down, poor thing), it is C; and finally, in the treble clef with no key signature, at the bottom, it is B natural (i.e. H in German).

And talking of crosses . . .

PART 5

Could There Perhaps Be a Story . . .
. . . *Behind* the Suites?

> God has preached the Gospel
> through Music.
>
> MARTIN LUTHER

It is with some trepidation that I embark upon this chapter. To quote Quintilianus (he who talked about preludes in Roman times) again:

> I feel weary at the very thought of the task I have undertaken. But I have set my hand to the plough and must not look back. My strength may fail me, but my courage must not fail.

Or something like that . . .

I realise that suggesting extra-musical associations for the suites will be anathema for some – maybe even sacrilege. However, I do think it's important to remember that for Bach, music and religion seem to have been inextricably linked – different aspects of worship that permeated his entire existence: Soli Deo gloria. Not for him the sort of Christianity so admirably described by the Victorian novelist Wilkie Collins in his novel *Armadale*:

I have noticed that the Christianity of a certain class of respectable people begins when they open their prayer-books at eleven o'clock on Sunday morning, and ends when they shut them up again at one o'clock on Sunday afternoon. Nothing so astonishes and insults Christians of this sort as reminding them of their Christianity on a week-day.

Bach's religious conviction was on an utterly different plane, as we can feel through both his words and his art; he seems to have believed with every fibre of his being, every day of the week, every hour of the day or night. It is reasonable, therefore, to assume that it was not just the works with sacred texts that encompassed his religious feelings; all of his music was likely to have expressed his faith, the cello suites very much included.

On the other hand, it is impossible to prove that there are specific religious (or other) associations within the suites – even though there is, I believe, some circumstantial evidence. It's also true that Bach's musical impressions of, say, the Nativity are unlikely to be clearly differentiated, in the absence of text, from any other deeply tender, gentle music in his output; the emotions are universal. Having started with that disclaimer, however, I have to declare that I firmly believe that there *are* religious connotations in the suites; this is entirely an instinctive feeling I have about the music, not a 'theory' – and in the hope that it may inspire some players or listeners to a deeper understanding of, or feeling for, the music (as I feel it inspires me, a non-

Christian), I feel justified in setting out the basis for these thoughts.

Before embarking upon my theory-which-is-not-a-theory, we have to take a brief look at Bach and numbers, and Bach and symbols. It is commonly thought that Bach had a great interest in numbers – well, we know he did, because it shines through all his works, with their perfect symmetry. I have already mentioned Ruth Tatlow's article about numbers of bars in the works for violin, one of countless examples in his music; surely they cannot all be mere coincidences? Since for most of his life Bach would have had to take a 'rastrum', or 'raster' – a nifty little device for creating five parallel lines – in order to write out all his staves and bar lines himself (or at least get his family or students to do it for him), he could very possibly have counted the bar numbers before he wrote out the music; and then, with his absolute mastery, he could have manipulated the music to fit any proportions he favoured.

There is much more to the question of Bach and numbers, however. First, there are the numbers considered symbolic in Bach's time: seven, of course, for the days of the week, but also – perhaps even more so – six, the number of days during which God laboured to create the world, as well as being the Trinity twice over. The revered status of six was nothing new; already in the fifth century, St Augustine had written:

Six is a number perfect in itself, and not because God created all things in six days. Rather the inverse is true; God created all things in six days because the number is perfect.

This veneration of the number could partially explain why it became customary for so many baroque and later composers to include six works in their collections – as in Bach's 'Brandenburg' concertos, keyboard suites, violin partitas/ sonatas, cello suites, etc. (Though I mustn't get carried away: to have six works in a collection also makes absolute musical sense, allowing the composer, for instance, to use half the notes in the octave as the tonic of the pieces in the set.)

It is hard for us to judge how many of Bach's supposed numerical references were actually intended; but we must remember that Bach was a man who could solve any musical challenge he faced, whether it concerned composition; acoustics (he could tell at a glance the acoustical properties of any building he entered); or the possibilities of any instrument – he would instantly produce sounds from an organ that, according to C. P. E. Bach, would make its builders turn 'pale with fright'. Bach was capable of any possible musical feat, in fact. A friend of mine, the harpsichordist and conductor Richard Egarr, once spent a whole dinner dazzling me with talk of the mathematics hidden within the 'Brandenburg' concertos and Bach's keyboard works. By the end of his peroration, I was dazed (and a little drunk). 'But – why?' I gasped. 'Because he could,' was the answer.

Then there's the question of Bach's name: not surprisingly, he would often incorporate the pattern of notes spelled out by the letters of his name within his works; he does so, significantly, in the unfinished final fugue of his last major work, *The Art of Fugue*. But also it is widely (though not universally) believed that Bach was intrigued by the numbers into which his name could be translated: if the letters of the alphabet are counted, with A equalling one, B two, etc., Bach's surname adds up to fourteen. 'J. S. Bach', on the other hand, comes to a pleasingly palindromic forty-one. (In Germany in Bach's time, I and J were counted as the same letter; in today's English alphabet his name would add up to the slightly less satisfying forty-three.) Some of the theories resulting from these supposed number games are highly convincing: there is one, for instance, that suggests that Bach added the words 'Credo in unum Deum' into the text of the 'Patrem omnipotentem' movement in his B minor Mass in order to bring the number of words to fourteen, with eighty-four letters (six times fourteen, seven times twelve), within a movement containing eighty-four bars – a number which Bach, unusually, writes into the score; this seems to me to ring true. Furthermore, it all ties in perfectly with the fact that the cello suites have, depending which way you count, either thirty-six – i.e. six times six – movements, or (since the fifth movement is always in two parts) forty-two – i.e. seven times six, or half of eighty-four. On the other hand, we should probably be wary of the faintly mad notions that surface from time to time, such as the one averring that, because there are exactly 1,283 notes in the first Prelude and Fugue of *The Well-Tempered Clavier* – spelling out the letters ABHC, if you apply the system above – it is an indisputable fact that Bach planned it that way . . .

Ultimately, even though it's true that these conjectures do sometimes spiral out of control, there does seem to be a solid basis to the more reasonable ones; and it's worth remembering that a feeling for mathematics was thought in Bach's time to be an important foundation for the art of music. As the composer and musicologist Andreas Werckmeister (1645–1706) – who was largely responsible for promoting the tuning system for keyboards known as 'equal temperament', resulting in Bach's *Well-Tempered Clavier* – put it:

> Musical intervals are nothing other than numbers and proportions and since God created and ordered everything in Numbers, Proportion and Weighting, so also must the musician, indeed every person, be diligent and study how to reproduce such marvellous Order.

Following on quite naturally from that hotbed of theories, there's the question of religious symbolism in Bach's music. We can affirm without any doubt that Bach was a pretty devout Lutheran. On his death, his library contained two enormous collections of Luther's complete works, as well as many other theological works and a heavily annotated Bible, one of the annotations in Bach's hand containing the telling phrase: 'Music has been mandated by God's spirit.' His use of religious symbols in the cantatas, Chorale Preludes, Passions, etc., ranges from word-painting (such as rising scales to represent the Ascension) to – it has been suggested – an actual representation of the Cross through the shape of the notes on the page.

The vast majority of his music was written for the church; as mentioned earlier, only in Köthen – where he probably composed the cello suites – was he required to produce almost exclusively secular music. Throughout Bach's six years there, he composed fewer than a dozen vocal works (only two of which have survived), almost all of them celebratory works for Prince Leopold's birthday or for New Year's Day. Leopold was a staunch Calvinist; and Calvin, though recognising the importance of music, had banned all instrumental and a cappella music from church services, considering that it would distract the congregation from the serious business of worship. At least Bach could attend the local Lutheran church established by Leopold's mother, as well as sending his children to the Lutheran school she had founded; but any devotional feelings that he might have wished to express in his music would have had to be implied – hidden, even. Not that I am proposing that he was a Shostakovich-like figure, sneaking secret protest messages into his works; but in the absence of sacred text or titles, any religious references would have had, by necessity, to be somewhat subliminal.

In fact, sacred instrumental music would have been nothing new. There were such pieces as Corelli's *Christmas Concerto*, for instance, composed in the late 1600s, to be performed on Christmas Eve; and there were also, more unusually, the 'Mystery' or 'Rosary' sonatas by Heinrich Biber, alluded to earlier. These extraordinary works consist of fifteen sonatas for violin and keyboard, concluding with a Passacaglia for solo violin. Although the manuscript has no title page, we know that the sequence represents the fifteen miracles, or mysteries, of the Rosary, because each sonata is prefaced with a beautiful illustration depicting those miracles. The accompanied sonatas are grouped into three sections, representing five 'Joyful', five 'Sorrowful' and five 'Glorious' mysteries; for instance, the first is (now) entitled 'The Annunciation', the sixth 'Christ on the Mount of Olives' (denoting 'The Agony in the Garden') , the eleventh 'The Resurrection'. Several of the sonatas begin with a 'Präludium', which is then followed by movements including dances such as 'Allaman', 'Courente', 'Sarabande, 'Gigue' – and a 'Ciacona' in D. It is highly unlikely that Bach would have seen these sonatas, since, as far as we know, the only copy was in a library in Salzburg – but not completely impossible that he could have heard about them. Bach's employer in Köthen, Prince Leopold, was a true music nut, who while on his travels spent vast amounts on tickets for the opera, and also on acquiring old music; he seems to have been thirsty for any musical information he could gather. A few years before Bach arrived in Köthen, Leopold had spent some time in Vienna. There is surely a chance that he might have heard tell there (or elsewhere) of the old master who had written sacred music for the violin. We will never know, of course – but maybe . . .

The Rosary is a specifically Catholic concept, and as such would presumably have been inappropriate for Bach's beliefs – even if he was later to write the B minor Mass (which, incidentally, is not really in B minor), described by C. P. E. as his father's 'Great Catholic Mass'. Anyway, the important question, whether or not Bach knew about the 'Mystery' sonatas, is whether there might be some elements of religious subtext, similar to Biber's, embedded within Bach's music for strings. In 2001, an extraordinary recording entitled *Morimur* was released on the ECM label. In the accompanying booklet, a violin professor in Düsseldorf, Helga Thoene, expounded her view that Bach's Chaconne for solo violin, from the Partita in D minor, was written as a memorial for his first wife, Maria Barbara, and that it contains references to several Lutheran chorales. The recording included a performance of the Chaconne by the violinist Christoph Poppen, intertwined with the relevant chorales sung by the Hilliard Ensemble. The ideas were controversial, and not surprisingly provoked a variety of reactions. I personally found the whole project stimulating and pretty convincing. I was particularly taken with the religious aspect of the theory, since the Chaconne – at least as I count it – contains thirty-three phrases, thirty-three being the supposed age of Christ at the time of the Crucifixion; and at the very least, the performance provided us with a fascinating new piece of music, the Chaconne sounding, although quite different, strangely haunting when combined with the chorales.

Professor Thoene also mentioned in her notes that she thought that the three sonatas for solo violin represented three of the major festivals in the Lutheran calendar: the G minor symbolising Christmas (the Nativity), the A minor Easter (Crucifixion and Resurrection) and the C major Pentecost (the Gift of the Holy Spirit). This really struck a chord with me, because I had always felt instinctively that the six cello suites were inspired by events in the life of Christ. I had first started to sense that possibility when learning the fifth suite, the dark loneliness of which always brought to mind the Crucifixion; and when talking about the sixth suite with my teacher Jane Cowan, who described the opening as depicting pealing bells, suggesting the Resurrection. Gradually, I'd started to think about the possible subtext of the other suites as well – the Preludes in particular, the dance movements developing the story, as it were, exploring different aspects of the narrative set out in those Preludes. So the thoughts behind *Morimur* felt somehow familiar – and encouraging. Also, thinking back to Biber's sonatas, I realised that, even if it was nothing to do with the Rosary, the overall pattern of the six suites, with the two minor-mode works in the middle of two groups of three, really matches the arrangement of the 'Joyful', 'Sorrowful' and 'Glorious' mysteries. True, the varying fifth movements of the suites – the Minuets of nos. 1 and 2, the Bourrées of 3 and 4, the Gavottes of 5 and 6 – suggest a grouping of three times two, almost like a hemiola of dances; but tonally and emotionally, I'd say that the suites comprise two sets of three. Perhaps Bach was showing us, through these contradictory groupings, that it is neither specifically two times three nor three times two, but a complete set of six suites?

Another, related, question that comes to mind here is whether Bach might have quoted, or embedded, any Lutheran chorales within these Preludes – particularly if he really did so in the Chaconne. This for me is an open question, which perhaps should be explored further; there are certainly hints in the framework of the melodic lines that could be heard as chorale tunes. The danger in searching for them, though, as in searching for confirmation of the images that I believe I see/hear/feel in the suites, is that one tends to pounce on any little shred of potential evidence and twist it to fit one's own ideas – as with any theory on any subject whatsoever. For instance, three notes in the suites that are the same as three notes in a chorale melody may be trumpeted as proof that Bach is quoting that melody. Perhaps so – but it could also very well be a coincidence; there are, after all, only a limited number of intervals in the scale. Similarly, I have been searching for correspondences between the vocal works and the suites, and believe that I have found many of them; but even if those correlations are real (which I certainly think they are), that doesn't *prove*, of course, that they are intended. There are certain gestures within Bach's music that we encounter again and again, in various guises; it may just be his 'handwriting', so to speak. But surely these connections, like those between the numbers of bars, are too many, and too deep-seated, to be wholly coincidental? See what you think ...

Suite no. 1 in G major, BWV 1007

The Nativity

So geht denn hin, ihr Hirten, geht,
Dass ihr das Wunder seht:
Und findet ihr des Höchsten Sohn

In einer harten Krippe liegen,
So singet ihm bei seiner Wiegen
Aus einem süßen Ton
Und mit gesamtem Chor
Dies Lied zur Ruhe vor!

So go ye there, you Shepherds, go,
That you may see the miracle,
And find there the son of the Highest
Lying in a hard crib.
So sing to him in his cradle
In a sweet tone
And with the whole choir
This song for his rest.

WEIHNACHTS-ORATORIUM (*CHRISTMAS ORATORIO*), BWV 248

G major, according to Mattheson, is 'suitable for both serious and cheerful things'; he goes on to describe it – quoting an earlier writer, Athanasius Kircher (1602–80) – as 'a true guardian of moderation'. It is also a key often associated with the birth of Jesus, used for instance by Corelli in the Pastorale of his *Christmas Concerto*, by Handel in 'For unto us a Child is Born' in *Messiah*, and by Bach for much of his *Christmas Oratorio*. It seems to me that 'serious', 'cheerful' and 'moderate' are all inherent characteristics of this, the opening Prelude of the opening suite. From the first notes, Bach produces from the cello a calm resonance that is somehow reassuring, comforting – as well as innocent. From this beginning, we embark upon a gentle journey: the first 'foreign' key that we encounter – in the second bar – is the subdominant, the key of the fourth note of the scale, C major.

Since I will refer often to the subdominant, both as note (the fourth note of the scale) and as key (e.g. C major if G major is the tonic, F major if the movement is in C major, etc.), perhaps now is the time for a short disquisition on its properties – as I see them, at least. There is no way of telling for sure whether Bach thought of the subdominant as a key of thanksgiving; but it certainly seems to possess that quality within the suites, and repeatedly throughout his music. Again, this is entirely an instinctive, emotional reaction of mine; but it would make sense. The subdominant has religious connotations in that it features in 'plagal' cadences – in which the concluding chords of a musical phrase fall from the subdominant to the tonic, as opposed to the 'perfect' cadence, which proceeds from the dominant to the tonic. The fifteenth-century composer Johannes Ockeghem is said to have been the first to use this harmonic device for a final 'Amen'; from there, it became standard practice at the end of sacred works, to the extent that the plagal cadence also became known as the 'Amen' cadence. And is 'Amen' not an expression of gratitude, as well as of acceptance?

So it seems to me that Bach is offering us, in these opening notes, a sense of tender comfort (despite the 'hard crib') in the choice of tonality, the sonority and the key relationships. Also in the rhythmic figures: the lilting arpeggios of these opening bars do seem to denote both praise and the gentle rocking of a ship – or cradle? In two of the most

strikingly similar figures assigned to the cello in the cantatas, arpeggios (albeit in B flat major) accompany the words
'Mein Wandel auf der Welt ist einer Schifffahrt gleich' ('My
sojourn in the world is like a ship's journey', from BWV 56);
and – in G – 'Sei Lob und Ehr dem Höchsten Gut' ('Give
honour and praise to the highest good', BWV 117). Kindred
arpeggiated figures appear in the recitative from the *Christmas Oratorio* sung to the text quoted at the head of this
section.

Another noticeable feature of this Prelude, as it approaches its triumphant conclusion, is the repeated use of 'bariolage' – a French expression meaning 'a mixed colour-scheme',
used in music for string instruments to describe a passage
involving two voices, one generally melodic and stopped (i.e.
the finger pressed on the string to produce the note), the
other an adjacent open string sounded repeatedly. It makes
for intriguing textures, the stopped notes contrasting strongly with the more ringing open strings, the bow undulating
between the two. Bach uses this device quite frequently to
express joy – for instance, at the opening of the cantata
'Gelobet sei der Herr, mein Gott' ('Praised be the Lord, my
God', BWV 129); or in an aria with, unusually, two cello obbligato parts, 'Lass mein Herz die Münze sein, / Die ich dir,
mein Jesu, steure!' ('Let my heart be the coin with which I
render thee homage, my Jesus', BWV 163, composed as early
as 1715). He also, strikingly, uses bariolage in combination
with arpeggiated figures in the aria 'Wir danken und preisen
dein brünstiges Lieben / Und bringen ein Opfer der Lippen
vor dich' ('We thank and praise thee for thy warm love, and

bring an offering from our lips to you', BWV 134). (No incense or frankincense, perhaps, let alone myrrh – but it's something.)

A third possible ingredient – and I hope I'm not straying into the realm of conspiracy theories here – may also be introduced at this opening. The distinguished Bach – and Haydn, Brahms, etc. – scholar Karl Geiringer (1889–1989) uses this example from the violin figuration in the aria 'Gebt mir meinen Jesum wieder' ('Give me my Jesus again'), from the *St Matthew Passion*, to illustrate Bach's use of the cross shape in music:

This, according to Geiringer, reproduces the shape of the Greek letter X, consisting of a diagonally descending line and a horizontal one – this letter supposedly representing the Cross. If that is the case, then could it not also be true of the opening of this suite?

Furthermore, many commentators have pointed out that Bach is acutely aware of the connection between the sharp sign – 'Kreuz' in German – and the Cross. And he has chosen the major key with one sharp . . .

So to sum up: we have here a gentle, pastoral tonality; an opening figure that is used elsewhere by Bach to depict a ship's journey, and praise; another figure frequently representing joy; and perhaps a message – or at least hint – as the narration of the suites begins that this story is about Our Lord of the Cross. None of it is proof, by any means – needless to say; nor will I be able to offer anything more substantiated regarding the rest of the suites. But it does seem to me telling . . . Listen to this Prelude – and to the other five (six) movements – and I think you'll understand what I mean.

Suite no. 2 in D minor, BWV 1008

The Agony in the Garden

Mein Vater, ist's möglich, so gehe dieser Kelch von mir; doch nicht wie ich will, sondern wie du willt.

My Father, if it is possible, allow this cup to pass from me; but it is not as I will, rather as thou wilt.

PASSION ACCORDING TO SAINT MATTHEW, BWV 244

The second is perhaps the most intimate and meditative of all the six suites. Whereas the arpeggiated figures of the first Prelude immediately set the cello humming and vibrating, this D minor Prelude is notable for its sparse texture – for the most part a single melodic line, with only two chords heard before the last five bars (more on those later). Bach seems to be emphasising the solitary nature of the music, the sense of an individual communing with him/herself. The suite opens with a series of rising questions before resolving, in the fourth bar, into a cadence on the tonic. (All the Preludes except no. 6, as well as many of the dance movements, begin by establishing the tonic in this way – by means of a cadence within the first bars.) Bach frequently uses the key of D minor to express tragedy; in that respect, if perhaps not in too many others, he is close to Nigel Tufnel of Spinal Tap, who calls D minor 'the saddest of all keys . . . it makes people weep instantly'.

'The Agony in the Garden', the first of the 'Sorrowful' mysteries, refers to the scene in which, after the Last Supper, Jesus goes to the garden of Gethsemane, on the Mount of Olives, in order to pray. Asking his disciples to keep watch, Jesus prays to his Father to deliver him from his fate – but 'Thy Will be done'. Each time he returns to his disciples, he finds them sleeping; 'the spirit is willing, but the flesh is weak'. Eventually Judas, 'having received a detachment of troops, and officers from the chief priests and Pharisees', arrives with lanterns, torches and weapons, and Jesus is captured. The rest, one can honestly say, is history.

We find D minor in several of Bach's settings of this

episode: for instance, in his setting of the chorale 'Mein Jesu! was vor Seelenweh befällt dich in Gethsemane' ('My Jesus! What suffering of the soul befell you in Gethsemane', BWV 487); both the great Passions also move into D minor at this point in the story. Therefore, I think it's fair to say that Bach associated this event with this key. Other aspects of this Prelude seem, at the very least, to be extremely apposite: the sparse textures, the questioning intervals, the air of contemplation. There are intervals similar to the rising ones with which this suite begins in D minor movements in various cantatas, such as an early one, BWV 155 (1716), in the opening aria (called 'concerto'), 'Mein Gott, wie lang, ach lange? Des Jammers ist zuviel' ('My God, how long, ah – how long? The grief is too much'); the aria 'Meine Seele sei vergnügt, / Wie es Gott auch immer fügt' ('May my soul be content with whatever God ordains') from the cantata BWV 204; and likewise an aria in B minor, 'Ach schläfrige Seele, wie? ruhest du noch?' ('Ah slumbering spirit, what? You slumber still?'), from the cantata BWV 115. (This last also has distinct echoes of 'Erbarme dich' ['Have mercy'] from the *St Matthew Passion*.) I think I can rest my case – at least regarding the emotional context of this Prelude.

And then there are the chords at the Prelude's end, mentioned above. These are a puzzle. According to Anna Magdalena, these are the chords:

This *has* to be a mistake; the second and third chords cannot be the same – it sounds completely wrong.

Kellner has the following, far more likely reading:

the difference being that whereas Anna Magdalena has the same A–E–D chord for both the second and third bars, Kellner has an F in the middle of the second chord. Curious that there are five notes in the final chord in Kellner's version – impractical on a four-string instrument. But that chord in the second bar – with which sources C and D agree – makes far more sense than Anna Magdalena's version. There is a chance, I suppose, that there were actually supposed to be just four chords, making it into a more conventional four-bar phrase – that Bach repeated the second chord by mistake, and forgot to cross it out; but sources C and D also have five – and it is musically satisfying, somehow, as it stands. It is enigmatic, however; there is nothing similar to it, not just in this Prelude, but in any of the suites. It is certainly possible that Bach expected the player, rather than playing straight chords, to improvise some sort of pattern around them; in fact, source D indicates all but the final chord to be played as semiquavers, implying just that. (Some people point to a similar passage – they say – in the Chaconne, in which Bach sets up a tessellated shape, and then, providing just a skeleton text, leaves it to the violinist to continue that pattern. But it really isn't similar: in this

Prelude, there is no such pattern set up. If the cellist is going to improvise here, he/she really has to invent the ending around the tonal framework of the chords.) I think it's significant that the three earliest sources agree, if not on notes, then at least on the fact that there are five long, held chords. But then, I always wondered what they might signify – if anything? And I have a tentative suggestion, which I myself find artistically convincing, even if I'm aware that I might be Bach-ing up the wrong tree (yes, I did say that). Could these chords be representing the Five Holy Wounds, the piercings that Christ suffered during the Crucifixion? It may sound far-fetched, but it would make sense of the melancholy grandeur of this ending, the feeling of time standing still. 'As thou wilt' . . . It's a thought, anyway.

Suite no. 3 in C major, BWV 1009

The Holy Trinity

Höchsterwünschtes Freudenfest,
Das der Herr zu seinem Ruhme
Im erbauten Heiligtume
Uns vergnügt begehen lässt.
Höchsterwünschtes Freudenfest!

Much-awaited feast of joy
which the Lord allows us to celebrate
in his self-built kingdom
to honour his Glory.

CANTATA FOR TRINITY SUNDAY, BWV 194

Or – the Ascension?

Trinity Sunday was an important festival in Bach's time, marking as it did the end of the first half of the liturgical year, the Temporale; and similarly, the C major suite can be seen as marking the end of the first half of the cycle of suites. In both this suite and the cantata quoted above – itself based on a secular cantata composed in Köthen – one is immediately struck by the joyousness of the simple descending scale in the opening movement: Bach is making a far from solemn pronouncement.

One of my – most people's – favourite Bach scholars, Christoph Wolff, has written (on the subject of a 'riddle canon' by Bach):

It creates the C major triad [C–E–G], the acoustically purest of all triads, which represents the natural, God-given, most perfect harmonic sound . . . It is this sound that symbolised the dogma of the Holy Trinity. Like no other combination of tones, the natural triad could make audible and believable the *trias perfectionis et similitudinis* (the triad of perfection and [God-]likeness) . . . the essential identity between the Creator and the universe.

It seems rather a lot for an innocent little triad, which can't even afford a flat – or sharp, for that matter – to bear on its shoulders. But here, with this wonderfully simple but bold opening, twelve notes consisting of a straightforward downward scale plus an arpeggio (triad), Bach makes a proclamation of such joy that we are transported instantly, irresistibly into a world of glorious elation.

I remember, all the way back in 1974, going to hear a recital at the Maltings in Snape – the home of Benjamin Britten's Aldeburgh Festival – at which Mstislav Rostropovich was going to give a solo recital, the programme to include the premiere of Britten's third suite for cello; this had been delayed for several years because Rostropovich had been forbidden to travel abroad, as punishment for his support for the dissident writer Aleksandr Solzhenitsyn. The programme was to begin, however, with Bach. The anticipation in the audience was immense, not least because Britten himself was sitting in the box. Suddenly, Rostropovich swept onto the stage, sat down and immediately launched into this C major suite, played *fff*. We shot out of our skins! But it made a point . . .

The descending scale is a fairly constant feature in Bach's music, generally seeming to denote celebration* – as in the cantata BWV 194 quoted above, or the cantata BWV 214, written

---

* Bach also uses descending scales at times to depict earthquakes and thunderstorms; but there is no mistaking those instances for the ones representing exaltation. (One is somehow reminded here of P. G. Wodehouse's perceptive observation that 'it is never difficult to distinguish between a Scotsman with a grievance and a ray of sunshine'.)

in honour of the birthday of Maria Josepha, Princess Elector of Saxony and Queen of Poland: 'Tönet, ihr Pauken! Erschallet, Trompeten!' ('Sound your drums! Resound, trumpets!') There is also a series of falling scales notably similar to those of this Prelude, and also beginning in C major, in the continuo part (including cello) near the opening of the cantata 'Jesu nun sei gepreiset / Zu diesem neuen Jahr' ('Jesus now be praised for this New Year', BWV 41); and there are many more celebratory ones at the opening of the Ascension Oratorio (BWV 11). (The scales seem to me to be going the wrong way: shouldn't they be ascending, rather than descending? But let it pass; maybe Bach was in that one way a typical man – no sense of direction.) In fact, the opening of this Oratorio is so reminiscent of the Prelude of the third suite, despite being in D rather than C major (they do seem to have been fairly interchangeable keys for Bach), that I wonder whether the Ascension, the second of the 'Glorious' mysteries, might in fact have been the inspiration here? It's possible.

The hill-like rivulets with which the C major Prelude then advances are also to be found in many vocal works, such as in the cantata BWV 173, to the words 'Nun wir lassen unsere Pflicht / Opfer bringen, dankend singen' ('Now we leave our duty, and bring offerings, sing thanks'); in the cantata BWV 129, written for Trinity Sunday – 'Gelobet sei der Herr, Mein Gott, mein Licht, mein Leben' ('Give praise to the Lord, My God, my light, my life'); and to the words 'Gloria in excelsis Deo' in the B minor Mass. They all seem to tie in perfectly with this Prelude, perhaps the most exciting of all six – an outburst of glad tidings.

Suite no. 4 in E flat major, BWV 1010

Magnificat!

Magnificat anima mea Dominum.
My soul doth magnify the Lord.

Or – the Presentation in the Temple?

> Joy is an expansion of the soul,
> therefore it follows reasonably
> and naturally that one could
> best express this effect by large
> and expanded intervals.

JOHANN MATTHESON

The original version of Bach's Magnificat, first performed soon after he arrived in Leipzig, was in E flat major; it comprised twelve Latin movements, with four German hymn interpolations. 'Large and expanded intervals' are in evidence almost throughout the work – as they are in this fourth cello Prelude. Like its C major predecessor, the E flat Prelude is full of simple patterns; but whereas the third begins with an immediate sense of proclamation, the fourth conjures up from its opening bars a sense of vast architecture. One thinks – or at least, I think – of a spacious church, its roof soaring towards heaven. The very first interval is a giant leap between the cello's lowest E flat, on the C string, to one two octaves higher on the A string; it is quite startling in its boldness (and thoroughly awkward to play). These two E flats form the outer limits of an expansive arpeggiated pattern, which forms the basis of much of the movement, interrupted only by some cadenza-like passages – like written-out improvisations – which serve to heighten the excitement. Similarly leaping arpeggios occur fairly frequently in the accompaniments to several vocal works, illustrating texts such as 'Jesus soll mein erstes Wort / In dem neuen Jahre heißen' ('Jesus shall be my first word in the New Year', from BWV 171) and 'Gloria in excelsis Deo' in the G minor Mass (BWV 235), as well as featuring prominently in the Gloria movement of the B minor Mass.

In a way, the architectural opening makes me think of the fourth of the 'Joyful' mysteries, the Presentation of Jesus at the Temple. Bach celebrated this major festival (known also as the Purification of Mary) with several cantatas; however, they centre around the story of the old man Simeon, to whom it was revealed by the Holy Ghost that he 'should not see death before he had seen the Lord's Christ'. Having subsequently seen the infant Jesus in the Temple, he blessed the Lord, saying: 'Lord, now lettest thou thy servant depart in peace.' (According to Luke's Gospel, a woman named Anna, also present, was of 'fourscore plus four years' – i.e. eightyfour, Bach's beloved number; 'she gave thanks likewise unto the Lord'.) This story inspired the canticle 'Nunc Dimittis', set by composers such as Tallis and Schütz, as well as Bach. However, although Simeon accepts death with serene gratitude, I just cannot hear anything but vital, pulsing life in this fourth suite, so I don't find that connection convincing – despite the familiar vaulting arpeggios for solo violin at the opening of one of the relevant cantatas, 'Erfreute Zeit im neuen Bunde' ('Glad time of the new order', BWV 83).

Looking beyond the Prelude at the rest of the warm, down-to-earth music of this suite, I wonder – although perhaps I am again straying towards the unlikely here – whether the number four might have been strongly on Bach's mind as he composed this work. It's a strange idea, I know; but maybe. The number four, if not sacred to quite the same extent as three, was important within the Christian religion: as well as the four ends to the Cross, there were four Gospels and, crucially, there were four Hebrew letters in the name of God (as well as four letters in the name of Bach!). Musically, however, it signifies something different, though perhaps related: thanksgiving (as already mentioned), the 'Amen' cadence featuring a fall – or rise – from the fourth to the tonic. It is the presence of this aspect that I feel strongly throughout this suite. Bach evidently loved the relationship of the fourth to the tonic – no tetraphobe he. (Tetraphobia – curious word – is fear of the number four.) My feeling is – as usual – mostly instinctive, of course; but there are a couple of events within the music that seem to point to the significance of the number, apart from it being the fourth suite. For a start, the subdominant is already present in the third bar of the Prelude, and even earlier in the Sarabande; far more surprisingly, the second Bourrée is exactly a quarter of the length of the first, whereas in every other pair of movements within the suites, the two are almost exactly the same length. (In some other pairs of dances by Bach, there are long and short couples; but as far as I know this is a unique proportion.) And finally, one single note that could be just a mistake, but which I find attractive as well as convincing, in the very last bar of the suite: the final bar (number forty-two!) of the Gigue consists, unsurprisingly, of notes entirely within the E flat triad – in Kellner, and in sources C and D. However, Anna Magdalena's copy has an A flat, the fourth, in place of a G, for the third from last note. This – admittedly a pretty typical cadential device, but unexpected in this context – seems to lend it a special feeling, almost like a plagal, 'Amen' cadence; a smiling thank you to God. Even if it's merely a copying error (though I hope it isn't), I love it.

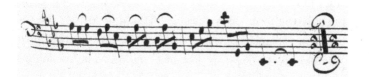

The ending of the Gigue, source C.

Anna Magdalena's version (with that wonderful A flat).

Ultimately, these are small details, however; even if Bach is giving us a few little hints about a subtext to the suite, they are of minor importance in the overall scheme of things. What truly matters is that through the towering structure of the Prelude, one can feel that Bach is setting up a temple in sound: Soli Deo gloria.

Suite no. 5 in C minor, BWV 1011

The Crucifixion

Crucifixus etiam pro nobis . . .

If a composer wishes to write a sombre masterpiece, he or she will often choose C minor; Beethoven, for instance, sets his fifth symphony, as well as his 'Pathetique' sonata and the last piano sonata, op. 111, in that key; Mozart's darkly hued piano concerto, K491, is also in C minor, as is his famous Mass, K427; Brahms' first symphony, Rachmaninov's second piano concerto – and so on. For some reason, it often seems to bring the very best out of composers. The tonality obviously meant something very special to Bach, the last movement of the *St Matthew Passion* and the final chorus of the *St John* being two telling examples of his use of it. For the cello, the key of C is obviously attractive, since the lowest note it can play (in normal tuning) is C. Having used the power of C major in a blaze of glory in the third suite, Bach darkens the sound-world of the fifth, not just by writing in the minor, but also by having the cellist tune down the top string, the A, to G. The result is extra resonance, as the top string now vibrates in sympathy with the third string, the G an octave lower – but also a sense of foreboding, of sadness, the natural brilliance of the instrument reduced. This sonority provides a perfect backdrop for the unfolding of tragedy: and tragedy is what Bach offers us, from the very first notes. The Prelude is conceived in the style of a 'French overture', a very popular genre in Bach's time (and one he used as a title for a whole multi-movement keyboard suite, originally in C minor: *Ouvertüre nach Französischer Art*, BWV 831). The basic form consists of a slow, solemn section featuring (double-)dotted rhythms, followed by a contrasting lively section, often fugal in nature. In some examples the first section is then repeated, but not here.

The impression as this suite unfolds is one of heart-rending narrative, the lowest C kept as a dramatic pedal-note, sounded or implied, for nine bars of darkness – three bars longer than the famous pulsing E underlying the opening of the *St Matthew Passion*. It is as if an Evangelist were setting out the story of the Crucifixion, recitative-like rhetoric interwoven with the dotted rhythms. Almost all of the first twenty-two bar lines of the Prelude are marked by chords – another of Bach's ways of adding intensity, in addition to emphasising the persistence of the pedal-notes. (There are similarities to some particularly dramatic chords in the cantata BWV 74, set to the words 'Leiden' and 'Sterben' ['suffering', 'death'].) The first section, as is customary for French overtures, ends on the dominant, in this case a three-note chord made up of open strings: G–D–G. It sounds curiously inconclusive, neither major nor minor – a questioning portal to the second stage of the journey.

Throughout his music, Bach's love of fugues is obvious; C. P. E. tells us that his father 'through his own study and reflection alone became even in his youth a pure and strong writer of fugues'. They thread their way throughout his output, from his earliest works, through *The Well-Tempered Clavier* (the forty-eight Preludes and Fugues in all the keys) to the monumental, unfinished (though barely) *Art of Fugue*. But why? Well, of course, they appealed hugely to Bach's monumental musical brain, always up for challenges; their mathematical properties were endlessly alluring to his questing spirit. But it is also quite natural to assume that for Bach, fugues – with or without religious texts, among the most astonishing of the former the several fugues within the B minor Mass – constituted a form of worship, an acknowledgement of the perfect order of the universe, an ideal way of demonstrating his view of the combined purpose of music: 'the glory of God and the recreation of the soul and mind' (the latter combined within one word, 'Gemüth').

In fact, the second part of the C minor Prelude, the only fugal section in the cello suites, cannot strictly be described as a fugue, since it is in one voice (unlike the multi-voice fugues for violin); but it is an 'implied fugue', with subject, counter-subject, tonal answer, etc. – all properties of a full fugue. It also suggests a constant sense of dialogue, reminding us of Forkel's description of Bach's performances 'introducing so much variety that every piece became a sort of conversation between its parts'. The structure is monumental, passing through cadences in the dominant, the subdominant – which throughout the suite seems to be linked to the relative major, both keys offering a gentler face to counter the forbidding aspects of the tonic and dominant – before returning to the original subject and thence home to C. It is all intensely dramatic, building up to a coda in which powerful chords, followed by challenging silences, culminate in a final so-called *tierce de Picardie* – a musical device in which a work in the minor ends in the major, in this case a four-note chord of C major.* Here, this transformative gesture seems to me to sound a bold note of affirmation, of faith. Bach uses the *tierce de Picardie* again and again – very often, as (I feel) here, as an avowal of his belief that Christ died for us, for our redemption. And this all sets the scene for the succeeding dance movements, which explore different aspects of tragedy in vividly contrasted episodes – at their heart, the famous Sarabande, the epitome of loneliness, desolation, despair. As suggested earlier, the voyage of each suite begins with the first note and continues uninterrupted to the last; but on a larger scale, there is also a feeling of a vast arc unifying all six suites within an epic journey. This fifth suite is the emotional low point of that voyage. It is also, I feel, the suite that tells

* Curiously, in the lute version the final chord is minor, but I suspect this is because the lute is unable to build up the same head of dynamic steam as the cello – and therefore the *tierce de Picardie* would not have the same effect. Similarly, the transposition from C minor to G minor for the lute would have been for a practical purpose, to accommodate the pitches of the lute strings.

the most clearly specific story: the Passion of Our Lord according to Saint Cello.

Suite no. 6 in D major, BWV 1012

The Resurrection

Et resurrexit . . .

In the B minor Mass, the bleak E minor of the Crucifixus movement suddenly, startlingly dissolves into G major; and then 'Et resurrexit' peals out in D major, the full choir joining forces with the full caboodle of trumpets (three of them), timpani, woodwinds and strings. It is quite a moment, to put it mildly – and not dissimilar to the sensation one experiences if one moves straight from the fifth to this sixth suite. The contrast in both cases is extraordinary – like emerging from the darkest of regions into the blazing sunlight.

The repeated notes with which this Prelude begins, triggering strong vibrations throughout the cello, are distinctly bell-like. We hear bells in several of Bach's vocal works; in many instances they represent death – but not always, by any means. A wonderful series of chimes, involving bariolage on three successive pairs of strings – similar to this Prelude –

occurs in the cantata BWV 133 'Ich freue mich in dir' ('I rejoice in you'), to the words 'Wie lieblich klingt es in den Ohren' ('How lovely it sounds in my ears'). Lovely it sounds indeed; and somehow it also *looks* lovely:

Further triumphant peals of repeated notes like these occur in the instrumental movements that open both the Easter Cantata in C, BWV 31, 'Der Himmel lacht! Die Erde jubilieret' ('Heaven laughs! The earth rejoices') – the first version of which dates from 1715 – and the *Easter Oratorio*, originally a cantata, in D. Both movements subsequently break out into exciting arpeggios, as does our Prelude. The spirit is remarkably similar – as it is in the repeated notes and flowing triplets of the organ chorale 'In Dulci Jubilo', from the collection *Das Orgelbüchlein*, completed in 1717. So I think we can assume that Bach was evoking a spirit of cele-bration, at the very least, with this Prelude; well, it's obvious – we can hear it.

Having darkened the sound of the cello with the tuned-down A string in the fifth suite, Bach now reaches out to the sky with a fifth string, an E string a fifth above the A – rather like those medieval master builders who developed Gothic windows, with pointed arches reaching towards heaven, letting in more light. It's as if Bach needs to climb higher in this suite than in the others, the music so full of joy that he needs more room in which to express it. This may make the lives of us four-string cellists harder, but it's worth it for the feeling of transcendent elation that this Prelude – and the rest of the suite – engenders. Christ is risen, indeed.

PART 6

Movement by Movement: Thirty-six (or forty-two) moments of perfection

Suite no. 1 in G major, BWV 1007

Prelude

When I ask friends to name their favourite movement from all the Bach suites, they often choose this Prelude. In a way, that surprises me, given the plethora of more ambitious glories in the later suites; but it is also understandable. There is something about those opening bars, the way Bach sets the natural resonance of the cello alight – but without the grandeur of the low C string – and the way he passes within those first bars from thanksgiving to dissonance, before returning to the comforting embrace of G major, that is true balm for the soul. The ending, too, with that long passage of bariolage creating anticipation before achieving the closing cadence, with its air of calm triumph – I'm sure that had he added dynamics, Bach would have marked *forte*, not *fortissimo* – brings a smile to the heart. I've heard people talk about the 'struggle' within this movement; well, I can't hear it. There is nothing in the harmonies to suggest real conflict, few serious clashes implied by the intervals. The music is radiant throughout.

One curious feature, which puzzled me for years, but to which I think I have (possibly) now found the answer: around mid-way through the movement (bar 22; track 1: 1′ 14″*), there is a fermata, or pause, marked over the high D that is held over from the second to the third beat of the bar; this is one of very few fermatas within the suites – and the others all come over notes that immediately precede rests, or at the end of the movement. Why this exception? It is not a full cadence or point of resolution – in fact, it sounds more like a question; nor is it exactly the halfway point. (There are forty-two bars in the Prelude; this pause occurs in bar 22.) But if I'm correct, Bach is encouraging us players – and, through us, our listeners – to hold that D in our minds for the rest of the Prelude: from there until the very final bar, were one to hold a bass note, it would have to be a D. That sense of dominant pedal gives the music impetus, encourages it to keep travelling towards the final, up-lifting arrival into the glow of G major.

---

* For many of the specific musical events discussed in this part of the book, I've included the relevant bar numbers for those of you who have a score of the suites to hand. For those who don't have access to the score, or who don't read music, however – and I hope that applies to a considerable proportion of my readers, since this book is intended for *everyone* who loves, or is interested in, the suites – I've also included the relevant track number and timings in (ahem) my own recording: *Bach: The Cello Suites*, Steven Isserlis, Hyperion CDA67541/2. (Suites 1–4 are contained on Disc 1, 5–6 on Disc 2.) Apologies for this apparent self-promotion – but I can't be sure that any other performer will feel the same qualities within the relevant passages.

Allemande

This flowing, legato movement inherits the radiance of the Prelude, albeit transformed into a dancing conversation. From the elegant opening upbeat and its resulting downbeat chord – a gentleman bowing a lady onto the dance floor? – the smooth lines reveal a world of serene benevolence, again unruffled by discord.

* * *

It's worth at this point outlining the basic form established in this movement, which continues throughout almost all the dance movements in the suites: there are two parts – both repeated – separated by a double-bar, with a cadence at that point into the dominant, or sometimes, if the movement is in the minor, into the relative major. However, it is perhaps wrong to speak of two halves since – often after a brief return to the tonic after the double-bar – there is usually a second cadence halfway through the second part, into a third key. A few of the movements (including this one, as it happens) also feature a cadence into a foreign key within the first part; therefore, these movements tend more often to be divided into three (or occasionally four) sections than two.

* * *

A minor detail, which may or may not hold any signifi-cance whatsoever: the cadence in the middle of the second part of almost every Allemande arrives on the third beat of the bar, giving it a certain lightness; the only exception

within the suites is the one within the second half of this
Allemande (bar 24; track 2: 1' 58", repeat 2' 49"), in the
rather unexpected key of A minor, which lands on the first
beat. Does that make it stronger? Something for the player
– and listener – to ponder.

Courante

This bundle of fun exudes energy and vitality, both through
the jagged opening rhythms and by means of such figures
as the exciting upward scales towards the ends of both
halves, in which the rising steps are placed – strikingly – on
the fourth semiquaver of each beat, lending it an eagerly
lurching quality (bars 14–15, 36–37; track 3: 1st part: 0' 22",
repeat 0' 53"; 2nd part: 1' 31", repeat 2' 11"). Had Bach followed exactly the pattern of the first half, the movement
would have ended at bar 40; but he gives us an extra two
bars, supplementing the elation, and taking this movement,
like the Prelude, to his apparently cherished number of
bars: forty-two.

The opening figure is curious, the 'melody' consisting of an
upbeat and then downbeat quaver, answered by two 'rhythm-
section' quavers played on open strings; the melodic line then
resumes from the second half of the second beat with six semi-
quavers, this pattern continuing with variations for the first
four bars. My teacher, Jane Cowan, used to describe it as a
portrait of a street entertainer performing an energetic dance
to the accompaniment of his pet monkey banging on a drum,
the second and third notes of each bar representing the drum-

beats. It's an image that has stayed with me . . . (and now it's in your brain too – ha!)

Sarabande

This is the first of the six immortal Sarabandes, the emotional centres of the suites. They function as the central slow movements (though as the suites progress, the Allemandes also become slower); each one moves us profoundly, albeit in rather different ways. In keeping with the rest of the suite, this Sarabande is tranquil, noble and touching, its gentle opening chords taking us within the first two beats from the tonic to the thanksgiving subdominant, C major. Again, the articulation is smooth, the dynamics obviously restrained. If this suite is indeed inspired by the story of the Nativity, then this movement must surely be a portrait of Mother Mary looking down at her sleeping infant.

This is the only Sarabande in the major that strays twice into the minor: a cadence into the relative minor, E (bar 12; track 4: 1' 37", repeat 2' 17") is swiftly answered by chords in the tonic and the subdominant, as at the beginning; but then the music poses a question in A minor (bar 14; track 4: 1' 47", repeat 2' 28") – which immediately, simply, melts back into the tonic. Double comfort.

Minuets 1 and 2

Bach contrasts his pairs of dances throughout the suites in various ways; in the case of these Minuets, it is not only the mode that diverges (the second being in G minor), but also the rhythmic energy, Minuet 1 beginning with a confident upward figure of two quavers and a crotchet (with a perhaps surprisingly strong second beat for a minuet), Minuet 2 with a three-note slur over three quavers, a far gentler gesture. The first Minuet seems bold and assertive, with several rising sequences; the second, particularly through the shorter ascending figures in the second part (bars 17–18, 19–20; track 5: from 1' 59", repeat from 2' 26"), questioning in nature. Both Minuets are twenty-four bars in length – a perfectly matched couple.

The distinction between these two Minuets provides a wonderful example of how Bach juxtaposes major and minor modes. The more introverted nature of the second Minuet is poignant, certainly, but it seems to me more tender than sad; the two movements are quite different in character, and yet – somehow – indissolubly united.

Gigue

If there is any air of poignancy lingering from the second Minuet, it is immediately swept away by the bold opening of this Gigue; I remember my teacher describing it as 'drunk'. She has a point, the slurred triplets of the first bar strangely contradicted by the staccato notes of the second. (Even Anna Magdalena, not normally prone to such things, seems to have marked staccato dots in that bar.) The spirit of this movement is rumbustious, but momentary shadows are still to be found, the unexpected hint of minor towards the end of both sections giving us brief pause for thought. This eclipse of spirits is soon eradicated, however, Bach adding a six-bar rising coda to remove all doubt.

(Modern) historical curiosity: when I was first learning the suites, it was for some reason customary to change the slurring at the beginning of this Gigue – and corresponding passages – thus completely altering the rhythm. In the opening figure, we were instructed to slur the first two Es and the first two Ds together, making the beats in question, as well as the matching passages, syncopated. Most odd – I cannot find any reason for this, but that's what some editions specified. It made it all sound even more drunk.

Suite no. 2 in D minor, BWV 1008

Prelude

From the first notes of the second suite, we are clearly in a very different world from that of the first. One of the challenges of writing for an unaccompanied string instrument is that the composer has to enable the player to provide the melody line, the harmony and the rhythm. The easiest way to establish the harmony is to include plenty of chords and broken chords – as in the first Prelude, with its many arpeggiated figures, which are in effect broken chords. Although this second Prelude begins with a triad of D minor within a rising fifth – D, F, A – the note-values are comparatively slow, so that it sounds more melodic than chordal. The intervals between the highest and lowest notes within these opening bars rise through a diminished seventh in the second bar to an octave in the third bar, before reaching a cadence on the tonic in the fourth. The whole phrase sounds like a series of three questions – or one question asked three times – with a final answer. As the movement evolves, it is almost entirely linear. Apart from the last five chords, discussed above, there is precisely one chord within the Prelude. The fragility of this texture evokes a strikingly intimate, inward-looking atmosphere – like a meditation. Rather than producing sounds from the cello that give the impression of a whole ensemble, as Bach does so often in the suites, here he emphasises the vulnerability of the lone voice. Of course, there is always a strong bassline underpinning the harmonic movement, but it is more often implied than stated. This Prelude is touching in a completely different way from all the others, a shared monologue that poses profound questions.

Towards the end of the movement, we hear that lone chord, in the key of the dominant, A major (bar 48; track 7: 2' 33"). (The dominant tonality of a minor key is a major key – curious, but true; and actually logical, because of the notes in the scale of that tonality.) Hearing the music approaching this cadence, the ear anticipates a simple dominant chord – A, E, C sharp. Instead of the A, however, Bach writes an unexpected G in the bass – or does he? Anna Magdalena's copy has G, as have sources C and D – but Kellner has a firm A. Which is right? Well, like the note at the end of the fourth suite mentioned in the previous section, I'd say that if it is a mistake, then it's a very beautiful one. It adds uncertainty, an even more searching quality to the chord; and besides, it is very possibly correct. Still, either version is quite feasible.

Allemande

Like that of the first suite, this Allemande is discursive, a continuation of the story begun in the Prelude. The mood is set here by the falling couplets, heard from the first bar, which lend the narrative a wistful air. It is the first example within the suites of a movement that dances, and yet seems to imply tragedy; Bach is already starting to stretch – without losing – the sense of dance to incorporate a far more profound emotional world than one might envisage from the appellation 'suite'.

An interesting feature of this movement is the addition of the one-bar codas with which Bach concludes both halves. A simple chord would have sufficed – he has already reached his harmonic goal. Instead, he appends to the first ending a phrase that, rising an octave, asks a question; and to the second an expressive answer, falling two octaves. These two bars considerably soften the effect of the final cadences, adding an extra layer of reflection.

Courante

There is far more assertive energy here, as befits a courante, the harmonic journey reaching the light of the relative major, F, much sooner than in the Allemande (which barely touches on it). Any suggestion of high spirits is dimmed, however, by the frequent descending pairs of semiquavers; they sound like sighs ...

. . . as do this Courante's most striking motif, the figures which Bach introduces towards the end of each half, a group of seven notes under a slur (bars 13–15, 28–31; track 9: from 0' 21", repeat from 0' 50"; 2nd half from 1' 18", repeat from 1' 47"). To my ears, at least, this sounds melancholy – far from what one would normally expect from a courante.

Sarabande

A grave, reflective movement, not surprisingly, autumnal colours abounding. Halfway through, however, we are afforded an unexpected shaft of light: a rising sequence as we approach the end of the first part resulting in a cadence – not in the dominant, but in the relative major (bars 8–12; track 10: from 0' 29", repeat from 1' 18"). This somehow feels like a moment of hope, a ray of tender understanding within the sadness of the whole. The corresponding sequence in the second half (bars 21–24; track 10: from 2' 09", repeat from 3' 14") – here rising not only in pitch, but also in texture, the chords progressing from two notes to three and then four – brings us further comfort.

Another memorable coda here (only at the end of the second part, not the first), this one extended over more than four bars. This is the only Sarabande in the suites to have such a coda, the other five reaching the end-point of their harmonic journey only within the concluding bar. Here, Bach takes the time to move from the lowest D, on the C string, up to one two octaves higher – a path towards the heavens – before coming to a final close back on that same low D. (Actually, Kellner's last D is an octave higher – but whichever: it arrives at a resting-point.)

Minuets 1 and 2

There is considerable strength, even austerity, to the many three-note chords with which the first Minuet begins, and – interspersed with some two-part writing – continues. It is all the more remarkable in the context of the suite heretofore, the Prelude having established such a monodic consistency. This fuller texture feels like a statement of defiance – far from the smiling elegance of the ballroom dance from which it takes its name. In utter contrast, however, is the second Minuet, in D major, which weaves its graceful path through a single line, not a chord in sight.

As in the first suite, this pair of Minuets are exactly the same length – twenty-four bars each; but here the acute differences are even more striking. It is not just a question of texture, but also of phrasing. In the first Minuet, the different phrases are clearly delineated, audible breaks between them. The melodic line of the second is almost continuous, the breaths between the phrases subtly camouflaged. And yet, again the two Minuets somehow form a completely satisfying two-part entity, Bach's divine logic working in mysterious ways – but working perfectly nonetheless.

Gigue

Of course, there is energy in this movement – how could there not be in a gigue? But the character is solemn nevertheless, the 3/8 time signature implying a considerably slower tempo than the 6/8 of the first Gigue. There is a strong sense of the story begun in the Prelude being brought to a conclusion, the connection emphasised by the opening intervals: whereas the Prelude began with a rising fifth and then diminished seventh, this Gigue begins with the same intervals inverted, now falling instead of rising – as if in answer to the questions posed by that opening. There is strength here, notably in the rising bass beneath couplet semiquavers in a four-bar phrase that occurs in both halves (bars 25–28, 61–64; track 12: 1st part from 0' 22", repeat from 0' 51"; 2nd part from 1' 24", repeat from 2' 06"). One gets the impression, if not of triumph – the mood is too sombre for that – then at least of resolution.

Bach leaves us with a positive gesture: the last two bars consist of a two-octave rising arpeggio, concluding on a high D. He could so easily – especially given the falling intervals that are such a feature of the work as a whole – have finished on a low D (as in the Sarabande), implying darkness, loss. But no – this is a decisive move towards the light: 'I will not leave you comfortless; I will come to you.'

Suite no. 3 in C major, BWV 1009

Prelude

I've already talked quite a lot about this Prelude, with its simple descending scale and triad ushering us into a world of celebration; but did I mention the marvel of the writing for cello, how the use of open strings – particularly the G string – sets the cello ringing, creating sonorities which sound like a vast string ensemble? Every note here vibrates with life, harmonically and rhythmically, the excitement heightened by such ideas as a rising figure with syncopated bowings (from bar 21; track 13: from 0' 42"):

followed by an electrifying passage with an open G string dominant pedal lasting for seventeen bars, the exhilaration increasing with every bar (from bar 45; track 13: from 1' 34"). Later, the Prelude approaches its ending with three spacious four-note chords, followed by long silences (from bar 77; track 13: from 2' 45") – rhetorical questions, to which the answer comes, without any reservation whatsoever: YES! And then Bach adds, for good measure, a coda that proceeds, via the thanksgiving subdominant, to a reprise of the opening bar. The bold challenge with which the Prelude began has been met, beyond any shadow of doubt; it is hard to think of any music more positive than this.

Forgive me if I get technical for a moment – but actually, it's not just a technical issue; it's musical – the two are in general hard to separate. There is another major bowing conundrum in this Prelude, at the beginning of the long dominant pedal passage. Anna Magdalena has been at the wine again (observe the slurs):

She seems to imply that in the first bar, the slur should be over the first two notes of each group of four, whereas in the second bar it is over the second and third notes for the first two beats, and back to the first two for the third beat; for the first two beats of the third bar, meanwhile, the slur appears to be over the first three notes, and so on over the page. Most odd.

Kellner's version is actually quite similar:

At first glance a little more stable, but not really: look at the second bar. One could also imagine, I suppose, that all this irregularity is actually an indication that the bowing is supposed to be varied; but since it's really not logical to make the same pattern sound so different every time – and Bach, for all his limitless fantasy, is never illogical – it seems highly unlikely.

Even source C – normally quite consistent – hedges his bets:

Only source D sticks to his guns – comparatively, at least:

And that – the slur over the first three notes of each four-note group – is how most cellists end up executing this passage. This, however, brings its own share of problems, because of course playing three notes takes up more bow than one, with the result that one may find oneself playing further and further up the bow; one can end up stuck out at the point, looking and sounding quite foolish. So we have to invent all sorts of tricks in order to avoid that happening – and all as we are attempting to convey effortless joy! See how we suffer for your enjoyment . . .*

Allemande

Following on from the ecstasy of the Prelude, this Allemande brings us down to earth (albeit fun-filled earth) with an elegant bump. As in the Prelude, the first complete bar takes us from a high C on the A string down to the low open C string; but instead of a dramatic flight, this is more of a slightly awkward walk, the lower octave almost seeming to give the impression of a dancer/walker with a rather large bum. Still, spirits remain high, if in a less elevated sort of way; and the Allemander saunters his way through the movement with a

---

* There is another possibility: John Butt suggests, convincingly (as always), that Bach sometimes marks slurs in certain passages merely to remind the player that the passage in question is to be played in 'slurred style'. Perhaps that is all that is meant by these various markings, and I/we should stop agonising about the exact placement of the slurs. But alas – I fear it's not *often* as simple as that . . .

contented smile on his face, plenty of rising sequences and hiccup-like outsize intervals contributing to the quietly ambling fun.

There is one touching little moment that it's easy to miss: after the cadence into A minor halfway through the second part, the music slides almost unnoticeably (bars 17–18; track 14: around 1' 59", repeat around 2' 48") into the subdominant, to which I repeatedly refer as the 'thanksgiving key'. (Maybe I shouldn't: as I've admitted, there's absolutely no proof that Bach thought of it that way; it's just that I feel that association so strongly throughout so much of the music.) It's a charming modulation – I bet Bach was smiling as he wrote it down. So many such wonderful touches throughout the suites; but one has to keep one's eyes and ears open for them. It was years before I noticed the beauty of this little musical twist. [*]

Courante

More high spirits here. Again, the first full bar takes us from the top C down to the low C – but here it leaps down by way of an arpeggio, laughing as it goes. Everything adds to the merry-making: hops between strings, rising sequences, pedal-notes, more awkward slurs. It's as if both Allemande and Courante continue the celebrations of the Prelude; but whereas the latter was a spiritual revelry, the two dances are

---

[*] Listening to that excerpt again, though, to get the timings – the first time I've listened to any of the recordings for many years – I realise that I could have played it much more charmingly. Apologies to Mr Bach. And to the record company. And to you.

assigned to honest-to-goodness, glad-hearted humans, continuing the festivities in the town, some distance from the church.

A really tiny detail here – but I love it. It's exactly the same modulation, and at exactly the same point, as the moment I mentioned in the Allemande: halfway through the second part, there is a cadence into the relative minor, A; then a little semiquaver butterfly semiquivers us into F major (in bar 56; track 15: 1' 28", repeat 2' 11"):

Such a lovely little flutter – also quite an eccentric one. Come to think of it, perhaps Bach had been at the wine too.

Sarabande

Radiant, serene, luminous – this Sarabande feels to me like a blessing, by no means quenching the joy of the previous movements, but elevating them to the realm of the transcendent. Again, the music moves almost immediately into the benediction of the subdominant – although F major is then not mentioned again until towards the end of the movement. Indeed, there is a moment of darkness, just before the cadence halfway through the second part. Moving towards D minor – rather than the expected relative minor, A – Bach gives us the dominant seventh of that key, consisting of the notes A, C sharp, E, G; then, on a syncopated long note, he

– 161 –

adds a B flat, fighting against that dominant seventh (particularly its A) in both harmonic and rhythmic terms, like an expression of pain (bar 14; track 16: 1' 43", repeat 2' 57" – plus my ornamentation that second time). But how he comforts us after the resulting D minor cadence. Leading us straight back towards the dominant, and then home – via an inspired little rising sequence (from the end of bar 20; track 16: from 2' 12", repeat from 2' 27") that passes again through F – the movement comes to rest on a quiet final cadence free from any uncertainty: a consecration.

The following is more about my experience than about the piece itself; but perhaps it will amuse slightly, just as an example of how little one can gauge the effect of one's performances . . . I have often played this Sarabande at both weddings and funerals, its unique magic seeming appropriate to both. It does seem as a rule to have a strong effect on listeners; but an event that took place many years ago has also stuck with me. At a summer course, I was sharing a flat with a pianist, who expressed a wish to hear me play. I agreed, and decided to play this Sarabande. It was a beautiful summer evening and, with the window open and the birds singing outside, I played, Bach's harmonies filling the room. At the end, I hovered for several seconds before lowering the bow; a special atmosphere lingered in the dusk, the pianist's soft breathing audible amidst the stillness. Then his voice broke the silence: 'Sorry – missed that. I had to take care of some soup in the kitchen. Could you play it again?'

Oh.

Bourrées 1 and 2

Moving from the exalted to the charming here, we have again two highly contrasted movements, the first Bourrée in an extroverted C major, presenting one of the most memorable tunes in the suites, the second in C minor taking us into a far more private world. This is not really a world of shadows, though – despite the minor mode, and one unexpectedly long D that sounds suspiciously like a sigh (bar 18; track 17: 1' 58", repeat 2' 24"). It is more as if the first Bourrée might represent Bach dancing with his children, the second portray him reflecting on his protective love for them; or is that too sentimental an image?

I'll try not to bore you with too much more bowing talk, but there is one section towards the end of the first Bourrée that has provided our four copyists with all sorts of different ideas:

Anna Magdalena.

Kellner.

Source C.

Source D.

*As you can see if you look closely, all four are a bit different
from each other; but here it's not really problematic, as it is in
the Prelude. One can choose any of them – the more eccentric
the better, as far as I'm concerned. All good fun here.*

Gigue

The revelries reach full throttle in this rollicking movement,
Bach throwing in lots of effects to heighten the jollity: bariolage, open-string pedal-notes, more smile-inducing modula-
tions. Right from the opening, there is no doubt whatsoever
that the movement will end on a high; and so it does, a C major
triad leading up to a four-note chord of C major for the last bar
– an upbeat downbeat, in fact, if you see what I mean . . .

*There's an adorably bucolic figure here which occurs towards
the end of both sections (bars 33–40, 93–100; track 18: 1st
part from 0' 24", repeat from 1' 03"; 2nd part from 1' 52",
repeat from 2' 43"): here the upper line plays against an open-
string drone, at times clashing against it in minor ninths or*

major sevenths (as dissonant as two notes can be) – as if a
band of folk musicians have wandered into the town square to
join in the celebrations. Party time.

Suite no. 4 in E flat major, BWV 1010

Prelude

And so we enter the second half of the cycle, with some more
joyous music – or perhaps the word 'glorious' is more accurate here than 'joyous'. I see this movement, as I suggested
earlier, as a magnificent temple in sound – an unadorned
temple, without any tragic images (or particularly colourful
ones) on the walls to distract us from the perfection of the
architecture. The scale is more spacious than in the previous
suites, as befits a place of worship. The first two suites present us with the initial cadence, establishing the tonic, within
four bars; the third requires six bars of dialogue in order to
answer its own question with a cadence; while this suite,
with its repetitions, makes us wait for eight bars before we're
assured that this is home. Again, our friend the subdominant
is the first foreign key to be heard; and once again, that produces (I feel/hear) a sense of particular warmth. The thrilling
effect of the opening is generated both by the low pedal E
flats at the beginning of the bar – nine of them – and by the
huge intervals between those E flats and the second note of
each bar, initiated by that astounding two-octave leap.

Having established itself in E flat major, the music sets out
on its journey with a resplendent walking bassline, moving
on the first beat of each bar, leading us onwards to the

dominant and beyond. At one point, the one-bar units expand to two bars – as if the welcoming Father is stretching his arms still wider (exciting to play, as well as to hear – from bar 27; track 19: from 0' 52"). Around the middle of the movement, a challenging silence confronts us (bar 49; track 19: 1' 38"); from this dramatic question emerges a long cadenza-like passage with an enormous slur over several of the bars – implying freedom of rhythm, as in most cadenzas. (This is perhaps a glimpse into Bach's improvisational style, as in the famous opening section of the *Chromatic Fantasia and Fugue* in D minor, BWV 903.) The extended flurry emerges, surprisingly, into G minor (bar 62; track 19: from 2' 15") – a comparatively distant relative of E flat. Although we have returned to the initial arch-like figure, it is now soft, tentative. Are we lost? Or are we perhaps merely standing in shadow in the middle of the temple? From this harmonic and dynamic low point, we move back gradually towards the elation of the opening; excitement and tension rebuild slowly, by way of some truly funky figuration, until we reach an ecstatic reprise of the opening, and a celebratory coda containing further multi-slurred cadenza passages. It is all thrillingly virtuosic – in a lofty sort of way.

That virtuosity, it must be said, presents some difficulties for the player. I've seen articles claiming that the suites become more difficult as they proceed; not strictly accurate. It's true that the first suite is from a technical standpoint the simplest of the six; this is quite normal in a set of six works, the composer perhaps seeking to ensnare the amateur who opens up the set, reassuring them with the musical butter-wouldn't-melt-in-its-mouth look of the first pages. (A clever trick.) The cello suites do become longer, certainly, as the set progresses, and more demanding overall; but it is not a completely smooth progression. Despite the scordatura of the fifth suite – problematic in itself – the work as a whole is still a lot easier from a technical point of view than this E flat suite – the only one of the set whose tonic does not lie on an open string. The entire work stretches the left hand of the cellist, in terms both of intonation and of the actual extensions involved; E flat is simply a tricky key for string players – it doesn't lie comfortably under the hand. (Mozart realised that, and specified that the viola should be tuned up a semitone for his famous Sinfonia Concertante in E flat for violin, viola and orchestra.) This Prelude is also famous for its memory traps; many's the unfortunate cellist (myself included) who in performance has desperately floundered their way to an unconvincing conclusion. I wouldn't say that the suite quite ranks with the notorious curse of Macbeth *for actors, but I do think that it comes close. When I was recording it, I'd invited a young Spanish cellist to listen to the session. I started the day with a playthrough of this Prelude; afterwards I conveyed with a certain verbal precision my view of the performance. My young colleague pointed out that she hadn't really learned anything from a musical point of view, but that she'd picked up quite a lot of new words in the English language ... But it's all worth it, of course; 'glorious' is truly the most appropriate word for this movement.*

Allemande

As at the corresponding point in the third suite, Bach takes us outside the place of worship for this Allemande; maybe, in fact, he is here focusing his camera on a rather simple member of the congregation walking home after the service, a light-hearted whistle on his lips. There is elegance too, of course, some of the semiquaver figures dancing quite gracefully within the beat; but the overall impression is one of extreme amiability – a parishioner who is satisfied with life, and not afraid to express himself to that effect.

Again, there are some differences between the bowings in the four manuscript versions, but they all agree in general that the prevalent rhythmic pattern is of sets of four semiquavers split into one and three notes to the bow, or vice versa. Many later editors, however, decided that this was all a mistake, and that what Bach actually meant was for the player to group all four semiquavers within one bow – i.e. to unite the whole beat under one slur – and they adjusted the text accordingly, making the effect far smoother. (As they did for several other movements throughout the suites: the fifth Sarabande suffers particularly from this 'ironing out', I think.) The editorial four-note slurs may sound prettier, but the more jagged bowings of the sources make the music talk, *not just sing. In this Allemande, the editors are wrong – in my opinion – to correct the lopsidedness. This just isn't smooth music. It needs to talk, gossip, burble – and the slightly rougher, less even bowing helps it to achieve those thoroughly praiseworthy goals.*

Courante

More simple fun is on display here, the music alternating between slightly hobnailed duplet quavers, cascading semi-quavers and good-hearted triplets. (Bach often seems to express a particular warmth through the latter – in his cantata BWV 85, for instance, an aria in E flat, 'Seht, was die Liebe tut' ['See what love can achieve'] is set entirely in triplets.) This is one of the funniest movements in the suites; if it doesn't bring a delighted smile to your lips, it's not being played properly.

There are further enormous intervals here; but whereas those in the Prelude seem grandly architectural in scope, these seem merely eccentric – tipsy, even. Could Bach be portraying some-one with hiccups? It wouldn't be unknown in music; in fact, there's a whole musical genre – albeit more to do with alter-nating voices than unexpected intervals – dating back to the thirteenth century, known as 'hocket' or 'hocquet' (French for 'hiccup'). Well, maybe that's going a little far, but the music does seem to struggle to contain its high spirits, the heel-kicking gladness of heart being emphasised by all the fun Bach is having with both pitches and rhythms. He seems to have gone beyond innocent red wine here; well, we are told that he liked to have a glass of brandy by him when he composed . . .

Sarabande

The Sarabande, of course, takes us back to the realm of the sublime – *all* the Sarabandes attain that quality; but the sub-limity here has a gentle smile on its face. The opening is harmonically surprising: although it does officially begin in E flat, the first bar feels almost like an upbeat to the second bar, in A flat, the subdominant. (All right, I won't mention 'thanksgiving' again; whoops – I just did.) The repeated dotted rhythms give a sense of spaciousness, as do the several bars of three double- or triple-stopped crotchets. The ending, too, is expansive, an extra four bars added to its equivalent at the end of the first section. Time stops, in fact, the last bar with its gently rising E flat arpeggio (with added D) leaving us hovering.

It's possible that the dotted rhythms are here fulfilling their traditional role of depicting royalty – Lully, for instance, uses them to announce (musically) the arrival of the king, Bach to anticipate the appearance of Christ. Or maybe (it's all too easy to see extra-musical associations everywhere one looks) they're just purely musical figures, stately and elegant in themselves.

Bourrées 1 and 2

I have already mentioned the extraordinarily disparate lengths of the two Bourrées – a scale of four to one; but there's also a strange set of proportions *within* the first Bourrée, the second part being exactly four times as long as the first. Is Bach having fun with the fourth dance movement of the fourth suite, perhaps? Just as striking as the disparity in their lengths is the extreme contrast between the characters of the two dances. In the first, we have perhaps the same cheerful fellow who ambled his way through the Allemande and lurched through the Courante. There are no double-stops here (just one four-note chord in the final bar); apart from the groups of four semiquavers under a slur, the articulation is basically non legato, a spring in its step. There are two brief but unexpected diversions towards the end into A flat – the fourth of the scale, of course (from bars 29 and 42; track 23: from 1' 04" and from 1' 25", repeats from 2' 04" and 2' 25"; da capo from 4' 08" and 4' 29") – before the movement draws to its triumphant conclusion. This is extroverted dancing, I'd say, showing off to the assembled company, whereas the second Bourrée is introverted – withdrawn, graceful, with a beatific smile. The articulation in the latter is far more legato, with a feature unique within the suites: the second beat is frequently tied to the third, giving the impression of the dancer's feet gliding along the dance floor. The relationship between the two Bourrées somehow brings to mind a couple, in which the man, though (in this case) deeply likeable, talks too much and thinks he's brilliant; whereas his wife says little, is shy and self-deprecating – but is the really intelligent one. I think we all know couples like that ...

*Actually, perhaps the wife has brought along an equally grace-
ful and gifted friend, because the second Bourrée is in two
fairly equal double-stopped parts throughout – more so than
in any other movement in the suites. The voicing is particularly interesting here, in fact, because the two parts, by means
of a descending scale, actually swap places at the 'return'
(bar 8; track 23: 2' 59", repeat 3' 13"), the upper voice becoming the lower – rather like partners trading places mid-
dance. Yet another unusual feature of this second Bourrée is*

the harmonic form: the first part – which lasts only four bars – ends in the tonic, rather than the expected dominant. This means that this opening phrase could be repeated at the end of the little movement; but it isn't – not exactly, anyway. It's a curious miniature example of a 'rondeau'. (The first four bars of the second Gavotte of the sixth suite similarly end in the tonic, but that phrase is treated differently.) Such a tiny movement – only twelve bars – but such a wealth of invention; well, as Forkel says: 'In every modulation [or in this case, non-modulation] of his instrumental work is a new thought, a constantly progressive creation.' So true.

Gigue

Back we go to swashbuckling fun; this is probably the most rustic of all the Gigues, merrily barrelling its way along, its proportions again unusually asymmetrical: ten bars in the first part and thirty-two in the second (forty-two again!). Composed almost entirely of slurred triplets, this is the only Gigue in 12/8 time – meaning four beats to a bar, giving the music yet more of that feeling of spaciousness that has been apparent all the way through the suite. The ending is eminently enjoyable: after an unexpected foray upwards into A flat (again) for just two bars (bars 31–32; track 24: from 1' 09", repeat from 2' 04"), a heart-lifting rising sequence, seemingly implying a crescendo, propels us towards the exultant conclusion to an exultant suite.

Of all the movements in the suites, this is the one with least variety in terms of rhythm/articulation. Not that it's in the least bit boring – far from it. But it does seem as if in general for this suite, Bach is portraying straightforward townspeople – 'merry peasants', as Schumann would perhaps have described them – and their place of worship. Even the Sarabande seems like an uncomplicated thanksgiving. It is music devoid of tragedy – in stark contrast to the suite that follows . . .

Suite no. 5 in C minor, BWV 1011

Prelude

So, from the light into the heart of darkness; for me, as I have suggested earlier, this is the suite most inescapably connected with Christianity: the story of the Passion. It would be hard to think of an opening more desolate – in its noble way – than that of this Prelude, the initial dusky octave Cs succeeded by a *parlando* narrative. I have already spoken* about the effect of the scordatura†, the normally brilliant A string

---

* I know that one is supposed to put 'we' in passages like this – at least, that's what most academics seem to do: 'we have already spoken of this', 'as we have seen', etc. I refuse! It always seems to me condescending. The truth is that I have said it, and it's up to you whether you agree or not.

† Many cellists – myself shamefacedly included – do not tune down the A string when playing this suite, meaning that we occasionally have to leave out a note in a chord. The reason is that tuning the string up and down during a concert can upset the cello. Furthermore, the string, confused as to whether it is supposed to be an A or a G string, may go out of tune quite quickly; and since one rarely plays the suite by itself in a programme, without other works surrounding it, it is safer to avoid the scordatura. I did, however, record the suite with the upper G string – playing on a different cello from the one I used for the other suites.

tuned down to a plaintive G, and of the frequent repetition of the cello's lowest note, the C, along with the many chords; but the discordant sounds within those chords, in conjunction with the stately dotted rhythms, also convey deep suffering.

On the first beat of bar 2 we have a diminished seventh – the most dramatic of chords – above that low C; by the next bar we have returned to the tonic, making, unusually, a three-bar opening phrase. From there, the Evangelist's narrative (if that is what it is) unfolds through a mixture of those dotted rhythms and expository, speaking passages under slurs. (By dotted rhythms, I really mean here double-dotted; I'd say that double-dotting is pretty much essential here, although it is up to each player to determine the precise length of the notes.) In complete contrast, and yet very much part of the same whole, is the succeeding 'implied fugue'. It's extraordinary how Bach manages to leave absolutely no doubt that this *is* a fugue, even though it is single-voiced. Compare the look of this excerpt from the fugue from Bach's sonata no. 1 for violin, the G minor:

with an excerpt from our single-voiced example:

I'd say we have the better deal – or at least the easier one. But Bach, with his supreme understanding of his materials, is just being practical: the violin, its strings far closer together than the cello's (and in baroque times burdened with far less tension than violins have today, feeling especially relaxed when played with the flexible bows of the period), is capable – just – of playing these massive chords without ruining the musical line. If cellists had to play a series of triple and quadruple stops like that, everything would grind to a halt. So Bach gives us the bare bones of a fugue; and of course it's wholly satisfying, taking us on a wide-ranging, emotionally compelling journey – a true Bach fugue, in fact. As Forkel puts it:

> No one ever wrote Fugues to compare with his; indeed, persons unacquainted with them cannot imagine what a Fugue is and ought to be . . . [Bach's Fugues contain] all the characteristics we are accustomed to in freer

musical forms: a flowing and distinctive melody, ease, clarity, and facility in the progression of the parts, inexhaustible variety of modulation, purest harmony, the exclusion of every jarring or unnecessary note, unity of form and variety of style, rhythm, and measure, and such superabundant animation that the hearer may well ask himself whether every note is not actually alive.

Well put, say I; and I might add that the main fugue subject here (first heard from bar 27; track 1: from 2' 06"), like so many Bach produced, contains a distinct element of dance. To quote Forkel yet again (useful man):

Even in Fugue, with its complex interweaving of several parts, he was able to employ a rhythm as easy as it was striking, as characteristic as it was sustained from beginning to end, as natural as a simple Minuet.

In order to create a fugue from this single line, Bach gives us here a lot of normal fugue-y characteristics: the subject, sounding like a conversation between two voices, answered by another statement a fifth higher, i.e. in the dominant. That in turn is followed by the first of many episodes, taking us through other keys – and so on. The tempo seems to be lively; in fact, the lute version has the marking 'Très vite' for this section (although those words may not be in Bach's handwriting). From first note to last is an enormous trajectory, a vast arc punctuated only by cadences into the relative major, the dominant and the subdominant, returning – via much build-up of tension – to the subject in the tonic (from bar 175; track 1: from 4' 46"), and thence to the coda, with more exciting bass pedal-notes, culminating in that great *tierce de Picardie*. It is a breathtakingly magnificent structure, combining intense drama with profound strength; somehow the effect reminds me of Debussy's remark: 'the form *is* the emotion'.

The cadence at the end of the return of the fugue subject (bar 183; track 1: 4' 55"), which launches the coda, presents some interesting (I think) questions. It is an excellent example of how Bach deliberately leaves us hanging by his use of implication rather than statement. (Sorry – I know this will sound dry on paper; but it wouldn't if I could play it for you!) The subject ends with a single, unsupported C on the A string (i.e. the piano's 'middle C', not the low one). So what is the chord that is suggested beneath that C, since there certainly is an implied chord? If it were a C minor chord, that would mean we had a full, 'perfect' cadence, a breathing-point; but the chord that isn't there is equally likely to be in A flat major, which would mean an 'interrupted' cadence – in which case the tension wouldn't dissolve at all, leaving us instead with a dramatic, unanswered question. Again – who knows? (I remember the famous French cellist Paul Tortelier discussing that very point on BBC prime-time TV in the 1970s – those were the days.) True, in Bach's lute version, he writes the equivalent of an A flat in the bass; so is that in fact his intention – a definitely interrupted cadence? I really don't think so; there are lots of added harmonies and extra voices in the lute version (most of which could be played on the cello also, but what's the point?), put there because they suit the nature of the lute. In this case, he could easily have added a chord (or just an A flat) for the cello underneath the C, had he wanted to be specific; but he chose not to do so. Nobody understood harmony better than Bach, of course – but also, nobody understood the nature of the cello better than he did; we can be quite sure that he knew exactly what he was doing by leaving that middle C without a bass. I believe that we should play it exactly as written – as an unresolved question, which lends all the more power to that wonderful C major affirmation on the final chord of the movement.

Allemande

The only consistently dotted/double-dotted Allemande in the suites – the 'French' style again (the French like their dots) – this movement is deeply personal, introspective. It is as if, the story of Christ's betrayal and suffering having been told by the Evangelist in the Prelude, we now hear from Christ himself, his meditations on the Cross. The first 'foreign' cadence is into the subdominant F minor, which, as I said (wrote) earlier, seems throughout this suite to be inextricably linked to the relative major, E flat – both seemingly oases of consolation within this tale of sorrow. So there is an element of light here – and wisdom, certainly. It is very different, I know; but might there be echoes of the viola da gamba's obbligato part, full of dotted rhythms, in the aria from the *St Matthew Passion*, 'Komm, süsses Kreuz' ('Come, sweet Cross')? This Allemande is very much its own intensely private self, however, its subtle, searching profundity reaching well beyond the scope of words.

Among many extraordinary intervals and harmonies here, one startling downward plunge stands out: the fall of an octave and a tritone, from G a fourth below middle C to a dusky D flat on the C string (into bar 26; track 2: 3' 13", repeat 4' 35") – that's an augmented eleventh. It is heart-stopping – and really seems to be evoking a particular image; the trouble is, I don't know what that image might be. I remember playing it down the phone to John Tavener (who adored the suites) and asking him; he agreed that it must be somehow symbolic, but was also unable to specify the exact meaning. Another unanswerable riddle? There's also an insoluble – for me – conundrum on the first beat of the bar before that (bar 25, rather obviously; track 2: 3' 08", repeat 4' 30"): all four sources write a G in the bass of the chord. It sounds most odd, both in terms of harmony and of voice-leading; I've always corrected it – as do most cellists – to a B flat, which means that we have a logical dominant seventh of the key to which we are being led, E flat. However, the evidence for the defence mounts up: not only do all four manuscripts have that G, but even the lute manuscript has its equivalent (D). It just doesn't make sense – or does it? Another question to worry me until I die (at which point I'm hoping I'll be able to ask Bach himself).

Courante

Dark energy abounds here. This is the only Courante with numerous chords, imparting a very different atmosphere from all its counterparts. I'm reminded here of some of the choruses in Bach's Passions, in which the flow of recitatives, arias and chorales is violently interrupted by the bloodthirsty chanting of the crowd (such as the first chorus in the *St John Passion*, also in C minor: 'Jesum von Nazareth!'). This Courante is also distinguished from all the others in the suites by being in 3/2 time, with frequent hemiolas to give it space – space for anger?

Perhaps the above description is a bit simplistic. It is true of the movement as a whole, I'd say; but there are subtler shades, gentler harmonies, at certain points – such as a cadence into A flat, which doesn't feel like a menacing key. It shows the range of palette, the layers of meaning, that Bach can encompass within a short movement. Instrumental music, free of text, afforded Bach unlimited scope for such subtleties; as Forkel (yes, him again – for the last time, with much gratitude) says: 'In his great vocal compositions, [Bach] well knew how to repress his fantasy . . . but in his instrumental music this reserve was not necessary.'

Sarabande

And now we come to the movement that, along with the first Prelude, has captured the world's imagination to the most profound extent. This Sarabande is simply a miracle: no melody to speak of, no chords, no particular rhythmic interest – so why do these twenty bars of music move listeners so deeply? One can point to features such as the pain-filled appoggiaturas, and the breathtakingly expressive intervals between the notes – not just adjacent notes, but also between the first and the last notes of bars, intervals whose dissonance one can somehow feel across the beats separating them: the major seventh between the G and A flat at the beginning and end of the first bar, the minor ninth between the C and the B natural of the second bar, and so on. These are in effect semitone clashes, warring tones that will not let each other rest, their conflict piercing through the intervals heard between them. Then there's the fact that the final note in many bars belongs to the chord of the next bar – extraordinary. There are surely resemblances here to the aria 'Seufzer, Tränen, Kummer, Not' ('Sighs, tears, sorrow, grief'), from the cantata BWV 21 (first composed in 1713, and revised in Köthen in 1720), and to the bleak 'Et incarnatus est', as well as the Agnus Dei, from the B minor Mass; but finally this Sarabande is unique, inexplicable – and should remain that way: a true sacred mystery.

Not surprisingly, this Sarabande has fascinated and inspired artists in every genre under the sun – most famously, perhaps, Ingmar Bergman, who not only named his final film, based around this movement, Saraband, *but also featured it in memorable scenes in one of his most celebrated masterpieces,* Cries and Whispers. *He uses the music beautifully, but – dare I say it? – I think he's got it wrong. Of course, it may well be my lack of understanding of drama, resulting in my missing the point of the relevant scenes; but it seems to me that he brings in the Sarabande at moments of reconciliation, of rare contact between people. It's certainly true that there's a sense of compassion in this Sarabande – the first part ending in the comforting relative major, not the more austere dominant (as it could have); but I do feel strongly that the music represents above all the epitome of loneliness, Christ's suffering on the Cross mirroring that of the whole of mankind.*

Gavottes 1 and 2

More recognisable dance rhythms return in this movement, the first Gavotte in particular with its many slurred couplets bringing the music from death to life, its sense of dialogue between two parts recalling the fugal subject in the Prelude. Almost all the couplets are falling, giving them a quality of lamentation; the focus of the story may have changed – but it's still the same story. Similarly, both Passions break into movement soon after the Death on the Cross: the moment of anguish 'Es ist vollbracht' ('It is finished') in the *St John Passion* and the words 'Aber Jesus schrie abermal laut und verschied' ('But Jesus again let out a loud cry and departed') in the *St Matthew Passion* are soon followed by arias filled with a sense of dance. In this first Gavotte, perhaps the most unmistakably tragic element is the descending scale, marked by the top notes of succeeding four-note groups, towards the end of the movement (from bar 28; track 5: from 1' 05", repeat from 1' 45"; da capo from 4' 13"). Tears, surely?

The second Gavotte is so extraordinary that it deserves a paragraph all to itself. Remaining in C minor, and constructed from the same minimalist textural material – i.e. a single voice, no chords – as the Sarabande, it consists almost entirely of sorrowfully flowing triplets. It brings to mind the famous description of the last movement of the 'Funeral March' sonata by Chopin (who worshipped Bach): 'Wind howling through gravestones.' Unlike that movement, however, this Gavotte is very much a dance; and again – as

befits the composers' different personalities – in contrast to
Chopin's nihilistic finale, the Gavotte affords us glimpses of
tenderness amidst the desolation.*

Gigue

It is a lot to ask of a gigue – to complete a journey of such
monumental significance; but, of course, in Bach's hands this
is no problem. As I said much earlier (but in case you skipped
that bit, or were so bored that you've forgotten by now), this
is the only French-style Gigue, a 3/8 movement filled with
dotted rhythms – in particular a dotted quaver–semiquaver–
quaver pattern, characteristic of such gigues.

Having said that, there is an extraordinary, and unexpected, feature here: a series, towards the ends of both halves, of
notes that suddenly hang suspended in mid-air, as it were
(from bars 15 and 61; track 6: 1st part from 0' 15", repeat from
0' 39"; 2nd part from 1' 25", repeat from 2' 15"). It is as if the
wind has been taken out of the sails of the mournful dancer,
the heart just too heavy for the dance to continue. The first of
these notes in the second part, a middle C, is on a syncopation,

* Curious coincidence: after I'd written this passage, I happened to see an
article by the pianist and musicologist Anatole Leikin suggesting that this
very sonata of Chopin's was inspired by the Bach suites. He sees in the first
movement of Chopin's sonata a connection to the Prelude of the sixth suite,
however, rather than mentioning any similarity between this Gavotte and
Chopin's finale. Still, the two points are by no means mutually exclusive; and I
am heartened by his suggestion that Chopin might well have known the suites
through his great friend, the cellist Auguste Franchomme – who had studied
with Norblin, he who produced the first edition of the suites – and adopted
ideas from them for his great sonata.

which somehow makes it yet more despairing; and from there it is all descent, to the final low C – the darkest note on the cello – with which this tale of grief takes its leave.

It may all sound rather depressing – but it's not, of course; Bach never is. No matter how tragic his message, his art is always ultimately uplifting. Maybe it's because whatever he expresses – and his music encompasses all emotions – that expression is always clothed in beauty. Here he follows Mattheson's precept (or Mattheson follows him, perhaps): 'Anger, ardor, vengeance, rage, fury, and all other such violent affections . . . must still have a becoming singing quality.' But it is not just a question of beauty, it is also that Bach allows shafts of light into the harmonies, the music's understanding, compassion and wisdom somehow comforting us, in spite of and beyond the bleakness.

Suite no. 6 in D major, BWV 1012

Prelude

Perhaps one shouldn't go straight from the fifth suite into the sixth; maybe one should wait for a couple of days, and then play it on the third day? Or perhaps I should tone down the Christian imagery for this suite, and simply revel in the jubilation of that opening peal of bells. For surely that is what is represented here: bells ringing in celebration, followed by their echo. Again – surprise, surprise – an entirely new world of sound, Bach setting the cello's entire body reverberating with his triplet bariolage, open strings alternating with stopped notes to create an extraordinary resonance.

This beginning asserts itself so unmistakably in terms of both sonority and tonality that this is the only one of the six Preludes that sees no need to establish its tonic with a cadence within the first few bars – no question here that we are firmly set in D major. From there, upwards we surge, to the dominant, A (bar 12; track 7: 0' 28"), and then beyond that, to the dominant of the dominant, E (bar 23; track 7: 0' 56") – the enhanced dominant to its friends, though in public we can also call it the supertonic. A trajectory of rising fifths, in fact, with the opening bariolage motif, including its echo, on both A and E. (Sounds like an emergency; and sometimes it is – see below.)

After that upward curve, we take a bit of a sidetrack through the relative minor (B), before arriving back at the opening figure, echoes and all, this time on the subdominant G (bar 54; track 7: 2' 11"); from there, it's mountain-climbing time, as we ascend to what feels like the top of the cello (even on a five-string instrument), urged on to the highest peak by a dominant pedal (from bar 70; track 7: 2' 51"). From this point there can be no other way but down; accordingly, we start to descend, the sense of progress nevertheless maintained, thanks largely to the persistence of that dominant pedal – now unheard, unplayed, but unmistakable. In fact, the excitement builds up again, to such a point that the music has no choice but to break into semiquaver arpeggios (from bar 85; track 7: 3' 39"), running all over the place at lightning speed, before finally returning us to a reprise of the opening – first, in an attempt to fool us, landing on the dominant, and then, gloriously, taking us back to the tonic (bars 90/92; track 7: 3' 43" and

3' 49"). It is all totally thrilling; and thereafter, for good measure, we are given a coda, featuring the movement's first chords, six triple-stops (as befits the sixth suite), all followed by rhetorical silences. And from there, the eagle that has swooped with us over the mountains deposits us gently – via a grateful subdominant – as we land softly back home on D. An eminently fulfilling trip.

Here I have to put in a plea for sympathy for us poor cellists who play this on a four-string, rather than five-string, cello. It's hard! Since we have no open E string, we have to overcome that hurdle by playing what should be the open E notes on the A string with our thumb, stretching out (and it's a long stretch) to play the alternate notes on the D string. And from there we have to climb much further; to say that playing this Prelude is tricky would be a bit like saying that walking backwards from London to Edinburgh, carrying an egg on a spoon while wiggling our noses counter-clockwise, is a tad awkward. Furthermore, we have to keep all that struggle hidden from the audience, since the music has to pass without apparent effort through our fingers to their eagerly awaiting ears; after all, it's not their fault any more than ours that it's difficult. Oh well – I suppose that bellringing is quite an effort for the bellringers, but one doesn't hear any hint of that labour in the sound. We must attempt to achieve the same untrammelled result – perhaps remembering Bach's own extraordinary keyboard technique, which, we are told, allowed him to achieve wonders of virtuosity while to all appearances barely moving his fingers.

Allemande

Another miracle: a movement that instantaneously rewrites the history of allemandes. This is the least obviously dance-like of all the dance movements in the suites, taking (in the majority of performances) more than twice as long to play as most of the other Allemandes; as mentioned earlier, Kellner marks it 'Adagio', sources C and D 'Molto adagio'. It seems, perhaps, more vocal than instrumental, a blending of aria and recitative. Conversely, its closest siblings are found within Bach's instrumental output: there are distinct DNA resemblances to the Allemande of the D major keyboard partita BWV 828, and to the Adagio from the Sinfonia in F minor BWV 1046a, written in 1718.

This Allemande is composed largely of demi-semiquavers, even hemi-demi-semiquavers.* It looks, at first glance, quite forbidding, at least to the cellist:

---

* As I said, American note-names – eighths, quarters, etc. – are somewhat simpler.

But no: the music emanates luminosity from first note to last, warmth and serenity flowing throughout, imbued with an air of sanctity. And in the little one-bar codas that end both parts, there is a genuflection to the subdominant; I won't use the T-word again, but it's there ... (At least one can't accuse Bach of ingratitude – although perhaps the Leipzig town council would have begged to differ.)

*From a performer's point of view, this movement is as challenging to bring to life as any movement in the suites. I believe that there are two things one must bear in mind: the first is that, if one is thinking in terms of the recitatives that the short note-values bring to mind, there must be a certain freedom within the beat; but it is at least equally important to remember that, even though the style may be vocal in nature, it is still an allemande. The way to make the music live naturally, I feel, is to be conscious that underlying the flow of the melody is the constant metric pattern of the dance: **ONE** two THREE FOUR / **ONE** two THREE FOUR. One has to feel this, to breathe in expansive, unhurried spans, perhaps imagining a moving bassline controlling the flow of the melodic current.*

Courante

A Courante that, like its counterpart in the fourth suite, kicks up its heels; but somehow these heels are shod in more elevated shoes than the peasant clogs of number four. It's still good fun, however, especially when Bach brings in, halfway through the bar, groups of six slurred semiquavers (such as the ones starting in bar 12; track 9: 0' 16" etc.), which give this 3/4 movement a temporary feeling of 6/8 – somewhat discombobulating, in an exuberant sort of way. It's uncomplicated music, although lengthy – the ending in particular stretches out longer than one might expect. One does wonder, again, whether Bach particularly wanted the movement to last, as it does, seventy-two bars – twelve times six.

It is all so exhilarating that the temptation is to play it really fast, virtuosically. Well, it's definitely virtuosic; but all the notes have to be clear, too, or the joy evaporates. Strangely, this movement contains one of the few major divergences between sources C and D, C containing lots of subtle bowing patterns (one and three within a group of four semiquavers, for instance), D – with which most modern editors have sided – begging to differ. The bow-twisters in C (there are many in Anna Magdalena's and Kellner's versions too) would certainly slow down the tempo a bit; if played too fast, those articulations would sound horribly scrambled. Another example of why it's so important to examine all the manuscripts in order to aid our interpretive choices – there are so many surprises lurking within every suite.

Sarabande

Another overwhelming example of Bach's transcendent genius. The fifth Sarabande – rightly, of course – captures imaginations with its haunting, magical strangeness; but for sheer melting beauty, there is nothing in the suites – in music, even? – to beat this sixth Sarabande. In complete contrast to its predecessor, with its stark textures, this Sarabande has chords or double-stops on the majority of its beats, giving it a heavenly breadth further emphasised by its 3/2 time signature and slow note-values. I myself see absolutely nothing tragic about this movement (others may well disagree); but the radiant inspiration of its thirty-two bars is as deeply moving as any tragedy.

The music is full of double-stops in sixths – surely the most comforting interval in music. I wonder whether Brahms, who became increasingly addicted to sixths in his later music, knew this Sarabande? He may well have studied the suites during the periods in which he had constant access to Schumann's music library, and again during his involvement with the Bach Gesellschaft. There were doubtless many reasons for his love of the interval; but it would be pleasing if the irresistibly consoling textures of this movement had contributed to his addiction.

Gavottes 1 and 2

And from that exalted peak to a pair of movements infused with an utterly winning, guileless charm. The first Gavotte boasts a jaunty, hummable melody, a piper sauntering through town, cavorting children in his wake. That same piper continues on his merry way into the second Gavotte; at one point the music sounds suspiciously like a musette, a type of dance originally inspired by a form of bagpipes played with the bellows. (Maybe something of a consolation for bagpipe players, for whom Bach otherwise wrote so little?)

This second Gavotte also boasts a form unique within the suites: a captivatingly amiable four-bar phrase is heard twice; answered, after a double-bar, by a different four-bar passage, it returns, before giving way to the eight-bar musette soundalike (from halfway through bar 12; track 11: from 2' 01"). It then reappears for its fourth and final appearance (the only marked da capo within a movement in the suites). This simple-sounding Gavotte is laid out, in fact, in a comparatively extended rondo form – A, A, B, A, C, A; but it is entirely unpretentious, as good-natured a dance as one could ever hope to encounter.

Another unusual feature is that the second part of this second Gavotte is the only part of a dance movement within these suites not to be repeated – if you believe Anna Magdalena and Kellner, who mark only the da capo/dal segno; sources C and D, however, disagree:

Anna Magdalena – da capo, no repeat.

Kellner – quite right, Frau Bach: da capo, no repeat.

Source C – hmm ... da capo AND what look suspiciously like repeat marks.

Source D – I agree with my friend Herr Source C: definitely repeat marks here, to keep the da capo sign company.

One just has to choose. (I go with Anna Magdalena and Kellner.)

At any rate, the whole double movement is deeply lovable, and deservedly popular among players of many instruments – even wind-players, who can't really play the double-stops or chords ...

... talking of which: I didn't want to mention it when talking of the Sarabande, since dragging in practical concerns to the discussion of such sublimity seems like sacrilege; but another difficulty for us cellists in this suite, particularly in the Sara-bande and these Gavottes, is the plethora of chords, especial-ly those involving the (usually) missing E string. Bach, with his practical mind, evidently thinking of the closer-together strings of a five-string cello – resulting in increased smooth-ness on the three- and four-note chords – inserts many more

such chords into this suite than into any of the earlier ones. This does cause us fifth-string-challenged cellists extra problems: maintaining the precision of the tempo, and the flow of the melody, is demanding when one is so often having to play several notes before the beat (as these chords have to be played). Well, one needs a responsive cello and a relaxed right – and left – hand, and then it's possible. Just.

Gigue

How do you complete the greatest cycle ever to be written for a solo cello? With a Gigue of bounding, irresistible, unquenchable joy and high spirits, of course. Bach gives us so much in this movement, summing up all the previous Gigues (other than the fifth, which inhabits a world of its own): there are exciting pedal-note passages, more folk instruments, more bells, impossibly huge leaps, and towards the end, a flight from the bottom range of the cello up three octaves, and down again for good measure (from bar 63; track 12: from 2' 33", repeat from 3' 42"). The music positively crows with triumph, rejoicing in the world and all its good things – there could not be a more fitting finale.

And, oh – the feeling one has as one reaches the end of the cycle of six suites, playing this movement! I remember blurting out to the audience at the end of my last cycle at the Wigmore Hall the phrase that had lodged immovably in my head as I approached the finishing line: 'The greatest music ever written.' One has – should have – the sensation, with the final flourish of this Gigue, of arriving at the end of an enormous, life-changing journey, one that has taken us through every possible region of the human heart and led us finally to transcendent ecstasy.

And yet, as for Bach: he probably wrote the last notes, signed his name, wrote his customary 'Soli Deo gloria', put down his pen and went out to rehearse, or to repair his harpsichord quill plectrums; or perhaps he settled down to a convivial dinner involving singing with his family and friends, his next masterpieces already buzzing around in his head. A true, unarguable, immortal phenomenon of nature, of creation. Ladies and gentlemen, I give you:

Glossary of musical terms

Keys (or Tonalities – means the same thing)

This may sound a bit complicated; don't blame me – blame Pythagoras, or whoever it was who codified the laws of tonality. Here goes:

There are basically twelve pitches in Western music. Let's start, for alphabetical logic's sake, on A (or A natural, as it is also known); the next note up is a half-tone, or semitone, higher: A sharp, which, on a keyboard at least, is the same note as B flat. (The 'natural' notes are white keys on the piano, the flats/sharps the black ones.) Next comes – quite logically – B natural. The trouble is that the next step, B sharp, isn't a separate note – it's the same as C; and conversely, C flat is the same as B. Thereafter, the pattern settles down for a bit: C sharp/D flat; D natural; D sharp/E flat; E natural. Then we get another half-step instead of a whole-step between the names of notes, so that E sharp is the same as F natural, F flat the same as E natural. The remainder of the scale is logical again, thankfully, ending on G sharp/A flat, before beginning again on a higher version of A. Confusing? Not really – one gets used to it very quickly. For an explanation of the reasons for this unevenness, excellent ones are to be found, written by far more intelligent people than I, in books or on the Internet. So if you're interested, you're welcome to look there; after all, this is a music book, not a scientific treatise!

In Bach's time – and really until the twentieth century, when things started to unravel gradually – works were composed in 'keys', such as C major, C minor, etc. These were based on the notes used in the scales of those pieces – scales being a succession of tones, starting on the note that gives the scale its name. Scales follow a pattern which to our ears somehow sounds logical. They can be 'major' or 'minor'; as a gross generalisation (though it does apply to these suites), keys in the major tend to sound more cheerful, minor keys more poignant. (That could, I suppose, be to do with how composers use them; but there does seem to be something fundamentally mournful in the sheer sound of a minor scale.) The most striking difference arises from the third note of the scale, the first to be changed between major or minor; whether it's a whole tone away from the second note (major third) or a semitone (minor third) powerfully affects the mood.

A scale in C major – the only key with no flats or sharps involved – consists of the notes C–D–E–F–G–A–B, and then C again, an octave (i.e. eight full notes) higher. C minor contains flats – B flat, E flat, A flat; these are listed at the beginning of each 'stave', or line, of the music. This is known as the 'key signature', and is there to remind the player to keep playing those notes, not 'naturals'*; a flat is

* Just to make life simpler, there are two separate types of minor scales, known as harmonic and melodic. A harmonic scale in C minor sounds

represented by the sign ♭, a sharp by #. These symbols are marked just before the note in question – if, say, a composer wants you to play F sharp instead of F natural, when there's no F sharp in the key signature. The altered notes are known as 'accidentals'; that sounds a tad alarming, perhaps – but it really isn't.

The *Tonic* is the first note of the scale – e.g. C in C major; the 'home' to which the music returns when it's time to do so.

The *Dominant* – so-called because it's very important in any scale, for some reason – is the fifth: e.g. G in the key of C.

The *Subdominant* is the fourth – e.g. F in the key of C

The *Mediant* is the third, the *Supertonic* the second, the *Submediant* the sixth, the *Leading-note* – or *Leading-tone* – the seventh. (Not that I use those terms often or at all in this book – but in case you're interested.)

A *Tonic triad* is a group of three notes, with the tonic as the lowest note, the third above it and the fifth above it – it sounds inherently satisfying, for some reason. (Possibly because the two upper notes are already faintly heard as overtones when the tonic is sounded – part of the 'harmonic series'; but that's another subject – and as I said, this is a music book, not a science book!)

C–D–E flat–F–G–A flat–B natural–C. A melodic one contains different notes on the way up and the way down: ascending C–D–E flat–F–G–A natural–B natural–C; descending C–B flat–A flat–G–F–E flat–D–C. I know I said that C minor contains three flats, including B flats – and yet both scales include B natural; but the three flats are in the key signature, not in the scale itself. Befuddled? You're not the only one. I'm beginning to regret having started this section.

So that's the minimalist introduction to tonality.

Now:

Metre/rhythm

Needless to say (though I'm saying it anyway), this is exceedingly important in music – almost all music. These suites being derived, at least, from dance music, Bach uses many different types of metres and rhythms. Some useful terms:

Bars: Gradually, in the years before Bach appeared, almost all 'classical' music came to be divided into 'bars' – i.e. groups of beats divided by vertical lines, known as *bar lines*. The ends of large sections, or of movements, were marked by two such lines, known as *double bars*, or double bar lines. In another gross generalisation, the first beat of each bar tends to be the strongest – but there are as many exceptions to that rule as there are locusts in Africa.

Beat: The units in which we count musical values; in Bach's music, there are two, three or four beats per bar. (I dread, as I write this, receiving an irate message from Mr Bletherpuss of Much-Binding-on-the-Marsh, pointing out that Bach used 5/4 in a Passacaglia or somesuch; but I can't think of an instance.)

Crotchets, quavers, minims, etc.: The names of such units (in British parlance). Crotchets often represent one beat – although beats can also be measured in larger or smaller units. Quavers last half as long as a crotchet; then, getting longer, we have minims – worth two crotchets – or semibreves – four crotchets. A dot placed after a note makes it fifty per cent longer – for instance, a dotted minim is worth three crotchets rather than two, a dotted crotchet one-and-a-half crotchets.

On the shorter side are *semiquavers* – half the length of quavers, of course; *demi-semiquavers* – half that; *hemi-demi-semiquavers* – half that again; and after that the names get silly.

Here they are, in Bach's handwriting:

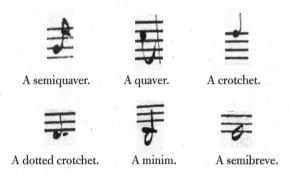

| A semiquaver. | A quaver. | A crotchet. |

| A dotted crotchet. | A minim. | A semibreve. |

Triplets: These look like minims, crotchets, quavers, etc., too, but are often written with a slur over them, with the number '3' placed under the slur; they are called triplet minims, crotchets, quavers, etc. The difference is that they are a third shorter than their duplet counterparts – so that, for instance, three triplet quavers make up a full crotchet beat, as do two 'normal' quavers.

Double-dotting: In baroque music particularly, it was understood that often (but not always – depending on the context) a long dotted note would be played longer than marked, a short one shorter; for instance, a dotted crotchet would acquire (roughly or exactly) an extra semiquaver's length, the succeeding quaver thus becoming a semiquaver (or thereabouts). This rhythmic device helps the music to breathe and dance.

Time signature: This is written at the beginning of each movement – and whenever the bar length alters, which can happen quite often in more recent music. (In some twentieth- and twenty-first-century pieces, in fact, the time signature changes almost every bar.) It indicates the length of each bar, with the first number – placed above the other – telling you how many units there are per bar, the second what that unit is (4 meaning crotchets, 8 quavers, 2 minims). So 3/4 = three crotchets per bar, 2/2 = two minims per bar, etc. Some time signatures imply groups of three: e.g. 6/8 = six quavers per bar, arranged into two groups of three; 9/4 = three groups of three crotchets, etc.

Simple time: Bars in which the beats can be divided into two, e.g. two quavers making up a crotchet beat.

Compound time: Those in which the beat can be divided into three, e.g. three quavers making up a dotted crotchet beat. (Seems to me that the opposite of 'simple' is 'complicated', not 'compound'; but let it pass.)

Hemiola: A pair of two bars with three beats, in which, rather than the usual strong first beat to each bar, the accents are on every second beat – i.e. 123123. It is often used in cadences (see below), somehow making the music sound more spacious.

Rubato (literally 'stolen time'): It's impossible for a composer to mark exactly the rhythms he or she wants. Listen to yourself or anyone else sing even the simplest tune; some notes will be a little longer or shorter than others, even if they're basically the same note-values. It's just natural. And that's essentially what rubato is: a little stretching of the time there, a little pushing of it here, preferably (in most music) around an organic, steady beat.

Expression marks/dynamics/tempo markings, etc.

Espressivo: Expressively.
Dolce: Sweetly.
Forte: Loudly.
Fortissimo: Even louder.
Piano: Softly.
Pianissimo: Even softer.
Crescendo: Get louder.
Diminuendo: Get softer.

(Not the most exciting section there, I know – but succinct, at least.)

Presto: Very fast.
Allegro: Fast (originally 'cheerful').
Vivace: Lively (not that it's relevant to this book, but some say that vivace was a slower marking than allegro in baroque times; that was later reversed).
Andante: At a walking pace (rather variable, depending on how fast/slowly you walk – or rather, the music walks).
Adagio: Slowly (originally 'gently').
Molto adagio: Very slowly.
Legato: Notes joined smoothly together, often marked by a slur over the conjoined notes.

Staccato: The opposite – notes clearly separated (sometimes involving the bow leaving the string, or the finger jumping off the key, between notes). This is generally marked by a dot (or dash/wedge) above the note(s) in question.

Pizzicato: Plucked, not bowed.

Forms

Fugue: Bach's master-form – nobody could write fugues like he could. It is a form, or genre, in which the main subject (or theme – basically the same thing) is first heard by itself, and is subsequently treated in all sorts of clever ways, reappearing in different guises and also interacting with any other melodic material the composer may wish to introduce (often in counterpoint, the combining of independent voices). Much, if not all, of the piece stems from that one chief subject, which has to be ultra-malleable – prepared to stand on its head, walk backwards, etc., etc. – but also interesting enough in itself to propel a whole structure. To add variety, the composer usually includes 'episodes', which are linking passages between different statements of the fugue's theme. It's an understatement to say that Bach relishes the challenge of creating these often vast edifices; no one in history has been as wildly inventive with their fugues as J. S.

Chaconne (or Ciaconna)/Passacaglia: Two forms that are rather hard to distinguish from each other. Both are entirely based on, or over, a musical pattern set up in the first bars, generally in the bassline; the difference tends to be (but this is another bendy rule) that the chaconne's basic figure will be more of a harmonic progression, the passacaglia's more melodic. Anyway, it's the chaconne that concerns us in this book, because of Bach's famous one for violin. Incidentally, the form may derive, like that of the sarabande, from a rather bawdy South American dance. No hint of that in Bach's masterpiece; well, children grow up . . .

Rondo: A movement in which the first theme keeps recurring at regular intervals, generally interspersed with at least two other themes or ideas.

Sonata: A work for one, two or sometimes three (as in trio sonatas) instruments, usually in three or four movements. (Pace Bach and Handel's born-in-1685 twin Domenico Scarlatti, who wrote over 500 single-movement sonatas.) In the accompanied solo or duo/trio sonatas of baroque times, the *continuo* – or bassline, assigned to the accompanying keyboard – would frequently be reinforced by an extra instrument, such as a cello, in order to make it more clearly audible.

Symphony: Generally a four-movement work for orchestra. (Bach didn't write any symphonies as such, but pointed the way towards them.)

Concerto: Nowadays thought of as a work for solo instrument(s) accompanied by orchestra. There are always exceptions to any of these terms, however; here it's easy to think of Bach's 'Italian' concerto, which is just for solo keyboard. And then there's the *concerto grosso* (by which the Italian concerto was inspired), which tends to be an orchestral work, with some soloistic passages for a few instruments. Furthermore, Bach would even label his cantatas as 'concertos'; but that's a different meaning altogether – there implying simply a collection of diverse forms within one work. When one mentions a concerto these days, however, it is almost always in that first sense – a solo work with orchestra.

Cantata: Vocal work with instrumental accompaniment. Can be religious (as most of Bach's are) or secular.

Oratorio: Also a vocal work with instrumental accompaniment, but generally on a larger scale than a cantata and (almost) invariably religious in nature, with a narrative element.

Sonata form: Not to be confused with a sonata – although often used in sonatas. A basic musical structure that became the norm for the first movement (and frequently for other movements as well) of multi-movement works in the years after Bach's death; but (of course) Bach managed to anticipate it. The three main sections of sonata form consist of the *Exposition*, during which one hears all the themes of a work, rather like being introduced to the characters in a novel; the *Development* (or, better I think, the German word *Durchführung* – 'moving through'), during which things happen to those characters – in this musical case the themes potentially being transformed in key, colour and mood, and sometimes combined; and the *Recapitulation*, where the themes return, restored to something like their original selves – a homecoming.

Da capo: Meaning literally 'from the head' – but in musical terms, 'back to the beginning'. This is marked in all the double movements – Minuets, Bourrées and Gavottes – in the suites; after playing the second of the pair, one repeats the first.

Compositional devices

Cadence: A cadence is an arrival in a key, or on a concluding harmony; it can give the same feeling to music as a full stop, semi-colon or comma – depending on the type of cadence – does to language. There are various categories, the chief ones being: the *perfect cadence*, leading from the dominant to the tonic; the *plagal cadence*, arriving at the tonic via the sub-dominant; the *imperfect cadence*, landing on the dominant instead of the tonic; and the *interrupted cadence*, in which the ear expects the chord to resolve from the dominant to the tonic, but it doesn't, often going to the sixth instead. Pleasure interrupted ...

Cadenza: A passage, usually for solo instrument, in which the beat is less strongly felt than usual. In concertos, cadenzas are generally free, unaccompanied sections for the soloist, not always composed in advance, and usually placed towards the end of a movement. Until well into the nine-teenth century, at least, soloists were expected to be able to improvise cadenzas, extemporising on the themes of the movement they'd just played.

Pedal-note (sometimes called just *pedal*)*:* A note sounded repeatedly – the expression derives from the pedal on the organ, played with the foot. These notes are often repeti-tions of the dominant – but not necessarily; there are also many instances of tonic pedals/pedal-notes (as at the open-ing of the fifth suite). They serve to heighten excitement or anticipation, or whatever atmosphere the composer is seek-ing to evoke.

Bariolage: A passage in which one voice is played on one string, with stopped notes, alternating with another voice consisting of a repeated open string; this is a sonority unique to string instruments, which Bach uses to thrilling effect.

Scordatura: The practice of tuning strings to abnormal pitches – i.e. not the usual fifth apart (in the case of the violin, viola or cello).

Tierce de Picardie: This is a device wherein a piece written in a minor key concludes with a cadence into the major – generally sounding a positive note. This was much used by baroque composers, and carried on into the nineteenth century. It may be common in the music of Bach's time, but every time he uses it, it's GLORIOUS.

Bibliography

I have mentioned a few books within the course of this text, but no harm in mentioning them again, because they are all wonderfully interesting. And there are many others eminently worth reading:

The New Bach Reader, edited by Hans T. David and Arthur Mendel, revised and expanded by Christoph Wolff (W. W. Norton and Co., 1999), a collection of contemporary documents charting Bach's life, is a joy.

As is: *Johann Sebastian Bach: The Learned Musician* by Christoph Wolff, a fascinating and more detailed biography (Oxford University Press, 2000). And now we have another book from him: *Bach's Musical Universe* (W. W. Norton and Co., 2020). My thanks to Christoph Wolff for permission to quote from his work.

Anything written (or, of course, recorded) by John Butt is deeply valuable too. His books include *Bach's Dialogue with Modernity: Perspectives on the Passions* (Cambridge University Press, 2010).

He also edited the *Cambridge Companion to Bach* (Cambridge University Press, 1997).

Other Buttiana include *Playing with History: The Historical Approach to Musical Performance* (Cambridge University Press, 2002) and *Bach: Mass in B Minor* (Cambridge University Press, 2008).

I always find the writings of Ruth Tatlow deeply absorbing. Her books include *Bach's Numbers: Compositional Proportion and Significance* (Cambridge University Press, 2015). This contains the astonishing collection of numbers I quote, somewhat dumbfoundedly, in my own screed.

A few other books proved to be very useful as I splashed around looking for information:

Dance and the Music of Bach by Meredith Little and Natalie Jenne (expanded edition, Indiana University Press, 2009).

Another book from the same (publishing) stable also proved very worthwhile: *Bach's Cello Suites: Analyses and Explorations* by Allen Winold (two volumes, Indiana University Press, 2007).

Other books about the suites themselves include an extraordinary tome written by one of the most belovedly eccentric characters in recent musical life, the – alas, late – Dutch cellist Anner Bylsma, whose recordings of the suites were perhaps the most influential since those of Casals: *Bach, the Fencing Master* (available at http://www.bylsmafencing.com/bach_the_fencing_master.html).

And one that helped to popularise the Bach suites further: *The Cello Suites: In Search of a Baroque Masterpiece* by Eric Siblin (Vintage, 2011).

Then there's a vintage classic: Albert Schweitzer's *J. S. Bach* (first published in French, 1905, followed by a two-volume edition in German, 1909; various reprints of Ernest Newman's English translation available). I'm sure that many scholars would take issue with some boldly stated facts here, but Schweitzer's love for Bach is touchingly evident.

Many other interesting books about Bach have also appeared in recent years, including:

Evening in the Palace of Reason: Bach Meets Frederick the Great in the Age of Enlightenment by James Gaines (Harper Perennial, 2010).

Music in the Castle of Heaven: A Portrait of Johann Sebastian Bach by John Eliot Gardiner (Penguin, 2014).

Then, a couple of fascinating (I think) sidelines: for those who read German (alas, I am not among them), a book about Anna Magdalena's life as a widow by my friend Eberhard Spree. Eberhard is a double-bassist in the Leipzig Gewandhaus Orchestra and an expert on the musical giants of Leipzig (Bach, Mendelssohn and Schumann), who has kindly taken me on two memorable 'Bach tours' of the city:

Eberhard Spree, *Die verwitwete Frau Capellmeisterin*

Bach: Studie über die Verteilung vom Nachlass Johann Sebastian Bachs (Verlag Klaus-Jürgen Kamprad, 2019).

From more recent history, there are many fine books written about Casals, all of which describe his love affair with the suites; perhaps the most popular is *Joys and Sorrows*, his life story as told to Albert E. Kahn (Macdonald and Co., 1970). My thanks to Martita Casals Istomin for permission to quote Pablo Casals's words.

Lastly – really off the beaten track – a biography of the strange life of Christian Reimers, the cellist who transported Schumann's accompaniments for the Bach suites (and very possibly his lost 'Romances' for cello and piano) to Australia:

Paul Blackman, *Christian Reimers: A Spirited Performer – The Life of a Cellist, Artist and Spiritualist*, available at https://christianreimers.wixsite.com/home.

I'm proud to say that that book came into being as a result of a speech I made during an all-Schumann recital in Adelaide – where Reimers lived for some years – in which I begged the audience to check their attics, just in case a copy of the lost works might be nestling there ...

During the preparation for this tome, I also dipped in and out of various articles, several of which I found online. I can't remember them all, so apologies to those writers whose ideas I imbibed and then forgot where I'd read them. But some I do remember distinctly are:

Introduction to the Bärenreiter edition of the Bach suites

– including the four earliest sources, and the first edition – by Bettina Schwemer and Douglas Woodfull-Harris (2000 – the edition I use, hopping between the different manuscripts like an insecure squirrel).

Introduction to Bärenreiter's new edition of the Bach suites (BA 5257) by Andrew Talle (2018).

And yet another introduction, written by Joachim Draheim for the first edition of what may be Schumann's accompaniment to the third suite (Edition Breitkopf 8431).

Then:

'Remaining Silhouettes of Lost Bach Manuscripts? Re-evaluating J. P. Kellner's Copy of J. S. Bach's Solo String Compositions' by Zoltán Szabó (2015), available at https://bachnetwork.co.uk/ub10/ub10-szabo.pdf – a spirited defence of the importance of Kellner's work.

'The Encoding of Faith: Scordatura in Heinrich Biber's Mystery Sonatas' by Daniel John Edgar (Ph.D. thesis, University of York, 2008; available at https://core.ac.uk/download/pdf/77022779.pdf).

'Bach's Bells: *Mors certa, hora incerta*' by Thomas Braatz (2012), available at http://www.bach-cantatas.com/Articles/BachsBells.pdf.

And in addition, I am immensely grateful to five invaluable Internet resources:

Wikipedia, of course – how did we live without it?

YouTube afforded me the opportunity to listen to performances of anything Bach wrote – including the cantatas,
shockingly few of which I'd heard before.

IMSLP, or the 'Petrucci Music Library', which gave me
invaluable access to all of Bach's works.

Questia.com – now sadly departed to the great ether in
the sky – which offered the complete texts of many interesting books.

And one of my favourite sites of all time: the Bach Cantata site – www.bach-cantatas.com. A veritable treasure
trove of facts, information and gossip about the beloved
Leipzig cantor.

(And finally, as a writer, I'm very glad of the company of
Word's thesaurus!)

Acknowledgements

When one has, with a sigh of relief, finally completed a book, one of the most stress-inducing tasks one still has to face is the Acknowledgements page. Of course, it's a pleasure to thank those who have been helpful; but the worry is that one will forget to thank people who deserve one's gratitude – and one inevitably does forget! So apologies to any person or persons whom I inadvertently omit from this section; I'm not ungrateful – merely absent-minded.

Initially, I would like to thank my teacher, Jane Cowan, and my sisters Annette and Rachel for passing on to me, when I was still a child, their deep love – worship, practically – of the music of Bach. On a more immediately practical level, I'd like to thank my publisher Belinda Matthews for her instant and continuing enthusiasm for this project, and also for her good sense in persuading me to take out some of the sillier jokes ('Steven – remember this isn't a children's book,' she reminded me gently). Also at Faber, I am grateful to Josephine Salverda for her near-saintly forbearance over my endless 'maybe-could-we-perhaps-might-it-possibly-be'-ing when it came to the proofs. Before that, Michael Downes was, as always, an understanding, gentle and expert editor, who even managed to put the umlaut over the correct letter of Spı̈nal Tap – not easy on a modern computer. Joanna Bergin was – as ever with my various projects – encouraging and patient.

My friend Aaron Mendelsohn in Los Angeles was kind enough to read through the book at an early stage, and then to call to advise me to remove a particularly tasteless remark. (You'll never know . . .) Another great friend, pianist/composer/writer/painter/committed Catholic Stephen Hough, dealt with my endless enquiries about various aspects of the New Testament with a blend of equally admirable erudition and tolerance.

Then, crucially, two masters of their craft read the whole book through at a middle stage, and gave me immensely helpful feedback. Actor, author, director, music nut, *bon viveur* and wit Simon Callow gave me nuggets of practical wisdom, talking from the much-needed perspective of someone who, although deeply passionate about and (self-) educated on the subject (he knows far more music than I do), is not officially a performing musician; and one of the most wonderful figures in the music world, the conductor, keyboard player, revered scholar and beloved eccentric John Butt, showered me with the fruits of his seemingly endless knowledge. Both men should have had better things to do, but I'm deeply grateful to them nonetheless.

No doubt some errors have crept into this book, but unfortunately, I can't blame anyone else for them. Instead, I blame pollution/climate change/chemicals in food for addling my brain. Any mistakes are certainly not my fault – obviously.

Finally, I'd like to thank Macadamia the cat, who owns my son Gabriel and his girlfriend Amarins, for not chewing up my hard drive.

Image credits

Portraits

Johann Nikolaus Forkel, 1749–1818 (*page 12*)
Music Division, The New York Public Library. (1813.) Public
 domain, available at https://digitalcollections.nypl.org/
 items/510d47dd-f704-a3d9-e040-e00a18064a99.

Carl Philipp Emanuel Bach, 1714–88 (*page 13*)
Pastel drawing by Gottlieb Friedrich Bach, around 1733. Public
 domain, available at https://commons.wikimedia.org/wiki/
 File:Carl_Philipp_Emanuel_Bach_(1733).jpg.

Francesco Alborea, 1691–1739 (*page 23*)
Wien, Österreichische Nationalbibliothek, Bildarchiv und
 Grafiksammlung, Porträtsammlung, Inventar-Nr.
 PORT_00155553_01. Public domain, available at https://com-
 mons.wikimedia.org/wiki/File:Francesco_Alborea.jpg.

Portrait presumed to be of **Louis de Caix d'Hervelois** (c. 1670–1759)
 and **Marie-Anne de Caix** (*page 26*)
Unidentified painter. Public domain, available at https://commons.
 wikimedia.org/wiki/File:Louis_de_Caix_d%27Hervelois.jpg.

Giacobbe Cervetto, 1680–1783 (*page 27*)
Painting by Johann Zoffany (1733–1810). Public domain, available at
 https://commons.wikimedia.org/wiki/File:Giaccobe_Cervetto_
 (1680-1783).jpg.

Robert Schumann, 1810–56 (*page 59*)

Drawing by Jean-Joseph Bonaventure Laurens (1801–90), photograph by DeAgostini/Getty Images.

Pablo Casals, 1876–1973 (*page 64*)
Portrait at Carnegie Hall, New York City, New York, USA, Bain
News Service, 1917. Photograph by Universal History Archive/
Universal Images Group via Getty Images.

Musical scores

Facsimile editions of the four source manuscripts A–D are available in
the public domain at https://www.jsbachcellosuites.com/score.html.

Extract from the Hugo Becker edition (*page 40*):
Reproduced by kind permission of Peters Edition Limited, London.
Edition Peters also publishes an Urtext edition, ed. Paul Rubhardt.

Extract from C.P.E. Bach's catalogue (*page 46*):
Bach, C. P. E. (1790) *Verzeichniss Des Musikalischen Nachlasses Des
Verstorbenen Capellmeisters*. Gedruckt bey G. F. Schniebes,
Hamburg, monographic. Credit Line: Library of Congress, Music
Division. Available at https://www.loc.gov/item/08033180/.

Extract from Altnickol's manuscript (*page 48*):
Altnickol, Johann Christoph: 2 Sanctus; V (4), bc , 1748,
Staatsbibliothek zu Berlin – Preußischer Kulturbesitz, Germany.
Available at http://resolver.staatsbibliothek-berlin.de/
SBB0000F03100000000.

Extract from cantata BWV 9 (*page 53*):
Bach, J. S. (1731) Cantata, BWV 9: 'Es ist das Heil uns kommen her'.
Credit Line: Library of Congress, Music Division. Available at
https://www.loc.gov/item/2008575929/.

Extracts from sonata no. 1 for violin in G minor (*pages 53, 174, 199*):
Mus. ms. Bach P 967, Staatsbibliothek zu Berlin. Available at http://
resolver.staatsbibliothek-berlin.de/SBB0001D75F00000000.

Other images courtesy of the author.

General index

Sinfonia concertante in E flat
major (κ364) 167
Mühlhausen 5
musette 190–91

Neefe, Herr 58
Norblin, Louis-Pierre 31–2,
183n
number symbolism 113–16

Ockeghem, Johannes 123
oratorio 204
organ tuning 92

Palestrina, Giovanni Pierluigi
da: Liber V Missarum 62
passacaglia, *see* chaconne
pedal-note 205
Pepys, Samuel 17
Pergolesi, Giovanni Battista:
Stabat Mater 62
Poppen, Christoph 119
Praetorius, Michael 80, 84
Terpsichore 80, 84
prelude 70–73
see also Index of Bach's
Works: cello suites: preludes;
and Cello Suites nos 1–6

Quintilianus 71, 111

Rachmaninov, Sergey 71
Piano Concerto no. 2 in C
minor, op. 18 138
Rameau, Jean-Philippe 79
rastrum/raster 113
Reger, Max 66

Reimers, Christian 60–61
rondo 203
Rosary 118, 120
Rostropovich, Mstislav 132
Rousseau, Jean-Jacques 83
rubato 200–201
rubato in tempo 100

Salzburg 118
sarabande 70, 80–81
Scarlatti, Domenico 203
Scheibe, Johann Adolph 10, 102
scherzo 82
Schober, Johann Nikolaus 30
Schuberth (publisher) 60
Schumann, Clara 60
Schumann, Robert 59–60, 59,
62, 65, 85, 173, 190
Romances for cello and
piano 60–61
Schütz, Heinrich 136
'Nunc Dimittis' 135–6
Schwanberger (violinist) 29
Schweitzer, Albert 15
scordatura 22, 206
see also Index of Bach's
Works: Cello Suite no. 5
Servais, François-Adrien 20n
Shakespeare, William 92
*All's Well That Ends
Well* 87–8
Macbeth 167
Much Ado About Nothing 88
Twelfth Night 88
sharp sign (*Kreuz*) 125
Shostakovich, Dmitri 117
Silbermann, Gottfried 9

Index of works